IF I COULD DO IT ALL AGAIN

J. R. KLEIN

Copyright © 2022 J. R. Klein
All rights reserved
No part of this book may be reproduced in any written, electronic, recording, or photocopying without written permission of the publisher or author.

Although every precaution has been taken to verify the accuracy of the information contained herein, the author and publisher assume no responsibility for any errors or omissions. No liability is assumed for damages that may result from the use of information contained within. The names of most of the people are as they were in life. A few have been changed to save them from embarrassment.

Publisher: Del Gato
Cover Art: Dandelion Tea
Library of Congress Control Number: 2022914242
ISBN: 978-1-7368101-5-6
ISBN: 978-1-7368101-6-3 (ebook)

For

My wonderful wife, Jeanne
My beloved brother, Roy (1946-2012)
My dear sister, Patti (1950 – 2020)
My sweet mother (1922 – 2022)

Also by J. R. Klein

Frankie Jones
The Ostermann House
To Find: The Search for Meaning in Life on The Gringo Trail
A Distant Past, An Uncertain Future
The Visitor
The Code
Quarter Rats
Times Like These

Contents

1. Origins
2. Bensenville and La Grange
3. St. Francis Xavier, Christmas Pageant, One Weird Sheep
4. Little League, Ice Skating, Halloween, and Blackhawks Games
5. Altar Boy and Father O'Gara
6. Working at my Father's Restaurant and my introduction to the Chicago Mob
7. A Paper Route, Breaking up the Boredom, Hooky, and a Very Bad Train Ride
8. Joe Coffee Drinker
9. So you want to be a Missionary
10. Working at Jewel and the Perfect Crime
11. Taylor Forge and the United Steelworkers Union
12. Circle Campus, the SDS, and Getting Drafted
13. Memorial Hospital
14. Turn-On, Tune-In, Drop-Out in the Age of Aquarius
15. Hope of the Castle and Driving a Hack
16. A Candy Factory
17. Baltimore
18. Baltimore City Hospital — Down Time
19. Johns Hopkins University
20. Cedarcroft and a Trip to Mexico
21. Finishing at Hopkins, off to Penn and MIT
22. Del Mar and a Trek up the Amazon

23. UCSD and a Second Encounter with Carl Galloway
24. Costa Rica and Nicaragua
25. Out of California and into Oklahoma
26. Houston — Out of Darkness and into Light
27. Epilogue — If I Could Do It All Again

1

ORIGINS

I was born in August of 1947 to a family of five children. My brother, Roy, who was named after my father, was born eighteen months before me. Both he and I were true baby boomers. I had two sisters, Patricia (Patti) and Mary Beth, born three and six years after me, and a brother Kurt, who was born three years after Mary Beth.

My father had returned from Europe in 1945, where he spent four years in Patton's 3rd Army. Though lacking much in the way of education beyond high school, my father was a man of considerable intelligence and because he had scored high on his military induction tests, he was sent to Officer Training School in the Engineering Corp.

Patton's Army was stationed in England and Wales for over a year waiting to cross the English Channel and move into France and over to Paris and then, if all went well, head east to Berlin. The engineers led the way for the Allies by constructing and reconstructing bridges and railroads that the German army destroyed as it retreated. When the Patton's army got to Berlin, the Germans had just surrendered. My father along with the rest of the American soldiers were put on troop ships and sent across the Atlantic to join the fighting in the South Pacific. Halfway across, the Japanese surrendered, ending the war.

Though my father hated the war (I cannot remember him talking about it even once when I was a child or later), he was in his element with his training as an engineer. Math was a gift for him; he spent most of his life when not at work tinkering and fixing and building things.

My father was born in 1913 in Pittsburgh, Pennsylvania. He was given the name Roy Charles in honor of the town Charleroi, which literally means Charles Roy (King Charles) in French. The name was chosen by his father, who drove a truck daily to the small coal-mining town in the southwest corner of Pennsylvania just above West Virginia.

The Klein lineage dates to the early 1800s in Pennsylvania. Christian Klein, my great, great, grandfather, the son of Johann Jacob Klein, was born in 1810 in Bernbach, Hesse, Germany. He married Christina Schneider, also from Bernbach, Hesse. They had a son, John Robert Klein, my great grandfather, who was born in 1864 in Pittsburgh, Pennsylvania. He married Annie Smith, who was born in 1868 in Glamorgan, Wales and who had migrated to Pennsylvania with her parents. Glamorgan is the southern-most county in Wales and was known principally as a coal mining region. It is perhaps no surprise that the Smith family settled into a region of Pennsylvania rich in coal mines.

They moved to Punxsutawney, Pennsylvania, where my paternal grandfather, Robert John Klein, was born in 1889. Punxsutawney at that time was primarily a coalmining area of the state. The family eventually moved back to Pittsburgh where Robert John Klein married Wilma Zimmerman, my father's mother, who was born in 1894 in Pittsburgh.

Quite a bit is known about the Zimmerman side of my family. Wilma Zimmerman's parents were John Zimmerman and Maria Christophori, who were born in Slovakia and Hungary, respectively, and married in Pennsylvania. John Zimmerman's parents, my paternal great, great grandparents, were Daniel Zimmerman and Susanna Schwartz. Both families date to the late 1600s and early 1700s in what is today Slovakia. The Christophori lineage likewise can be traced to the same time frame in Slovakia and Hungary. I never met Wilma Zimmerman, my paternal grandmother. She died at the age of 47 in 1941 before I was born.

My father's family was large but typical for those days, consisting of four boys (Robert, Roy, Larry, and Eddie) and three girls (Olive, Frances, and Marie). When John Zimmerman died in 1916, his wife Maria moved in with the family, expanding it to ten people.

Robert John Klein spent much of his adult life working as a truck driver, reportedly having one of the first driver's licenses in the state. Though I met him only a few times, I remember that he was a fun and affable person. I recall that he once showed up at our house in La Grange outside Chicago when I was about five years old. He had driven from Pittsburgh and stayed with us for several months. According to my mother, he liked to cook, as did she, and he had brought with him an elegant set of copper cookware. As she later related to me, she met my father at the door one night when he came from work and told him: "Roy, your father can stay here as long as he likes. But we cannot both cook in the kitchen at the same time." My father said he would relay the message.

Throughout my grandfather's life, he was a supporter of issues that affected the working class. I feel quite certain that my grandfather's sense of social justice rubbed off on most of his children; I remember quite well how Uncle Bob and my father would talk about such things when he came to visit us.

My mother, Mary Elizabeth (Harris) Klein, was born in 1922. She celebrated her one hundredth birthday in May of 2022.

While I know a lot about my father's side of the family, I know almost nothing about my mother's side except that her biological father was an Irish immigrant and that she was raised by an English man who married my mother's mother. Interestingly, most of what I learned about my father's family came from my mother. My father never talked much about it, though he apparently related incidents of his childhood and young life to her.

Both my parents grew up in the depth of the Depression. While my father's family consisted of nine people in all and were extremely poor, my mother was an only child. She tells how for her school lunch sandwich she was fortunate to have a slice of ham, though for many of her friends a mustard sandwich was common. My father told my mother about 'midnight moves' that occurred when he was a boy. If his parents were behind on rent and threatened with eviction, they would rouse the children from bed late at night, pack a few suitcases, and head off to a new place.

Just as with the strong sense of social justice of my father's family, a similar thread existed in my mother her whole life, mostly generated from her own experiences as a child. She told me how, growing up in Cleveland, it was common to see signs in store windows that read: *Help Wanted, Irish Need Not Apply*. The Irish were viewed as lazy and excessively fond of alcohol. Of course, knowing that her own father was Irish must have made the effect of experiencing such discrimination even more painful.

Chicago at the time I was growing up was, and still is, a city of immigrants of every imaginable kind. Reportedly, there are around a hundred and sixty languages spoken in Chicago. The immigrant groups that stand out most from my childhood days were the people that had come from

Central and Eastern Europe—from Poland, Bohemia, which is part of the Czech Republic today, Hungary, and Germany, as well as Italians and Irish. The food consisted of diverse cuisines from those countries and many others.

Chicago is a place people have flocked to for work for centuries. As Carl Sandburg described in his epic poem:

Chicago—
Hog Butcher for the World
Tool Maker, Stacker of Wheat
Player with Railroads and the Nations
　Freight Handler...

The massive Union Stock Yards drew Italian and Irish workers. Politicians like Mayor Daley kept the city running like a well-oiled machine. It was a unique design in which the city was, and still is, divided into fifty wards, each headed by an alderman. When you needed something fixed or repaired in your ward—a streetlamp that was out, garbage that had not been picked up—you didn't place a call to some inchoate office at city hall. Instead, you dialed up your alderman and before you knew it, the problem was taken care of.

But, of course, one hand always washes the other. Aldermen were usually businesspeople of one type or another: an insurance salesman, a shop owner, a car dealer. They were rewarded with business from the residents of their ward. Each alderman was also responsible for rounding up a thousand votes for the mayor or for anyone else who was running for office, provided they were a Democrat, of course. These were legitimate votes, but the net effect was that it guaranteed a buffer of fifty thousand legal, honest votes at election time. It was a system that had been put in place long before Daley became mayor, but he perfected it.

2

BENSENVILLE AND LA GRANGE

My parents settled briefly in Cleveland when my father returned from Europe at the end of the Second World War. They left Cleveland and went to Detroit, where I was born, but stayed little more than a year. Moving again, they settled into Bensenville, Illinois, a northwest suburb of Chicago near what is today O'Hare Airport.

My first memory of life was when I was about three years old, maybe even younger. I remember standing on the corner down at the end of the street with my brother, Roy, who was a year older. A hole was being dug. A deep hole that was probably destined to be the basement of one of the many new houses that were rapidly being put up for the families of GIs after the war.

We were watching in awe as a tractor pulled load after load of dirt from the ground and dumped it in a pile next to the hole. A couple of other kids were with us, all about our age. There were no parents in sight, an almost unthinkable thing today. Imagine letting your three- or four-year-old wander down the street by themselves. But that's how it was then, and no one thought anything of it…apparently.

Suddenly, the tractor came climbing out of the hole with a massive load of dirt in the bucket. It swung toward us and lumbered in our direction. It was coming straight at us, or that's what it seemed like. All I remember was standing frozen, watching as it moved closer. Bursting into tears, convinced I was about to be forever buried under a mountain of dirt and clay, I turned and ran down the street—crying, petrified, freaked out with terror. It is an image that is forever seared into my memory.

Our house at that time was simple. It still exists today in Bensenville; it has changed very little. Square, red brick, built just after the Second World War. Uncle Sam slapped them together in record breaking time and no one was happier about it than people like my parents; this was their chance at the American Dream.

My father had a job in Chicago. He took the commuter train in and back every day and was home most nights for dinner. It was sometime during those days in Bensenville that my curiosity about science arose and I performed my first experiment ever. This was not done using an erector set or mixing harmless elements together from a chemistry set. Rather, I wanted to prove to myself that corn grew on stalks from kernels of corn.

One night at dinner, the topic came up. Who knows, we were probably eating corn on the cob fresh from a farm stand. In any event, it wasn't enough just to be told that corn—that whole stalks in fact—sprouted from small kernels. I had to prove it to myself.

Into the ground went a half dozen kernels right in the front of the house. Two months later we were the only house on the block with a row of six-foot high corn stalks looming out front. I had what I needed to prove what I had been told and now I believed it.

Bensenville had been grand but I remember almost nothing more about it other than the dreadful day I was attacked by a massive bulldozer and my success at growing towering cornstalks in the front yard.

My parents decided that my father needed to be closer to the city, so La Grange became our next stop. It was there that the person I was destined to be emerged—a very odd amalgam of good and bad, kind and generous, devious and resourceful—a sort of Jekyll and Hyde chimera of Wally Cleaver and Eddie Haskell all rolled into one.

La Grange was a nice place. Quaint, peaceful, and on the Burlington route that ran from Aurora to Union Station in downtown Chicago. My parents bought a house at 425 South Stone Avenue—a five bedroom, thirteen room Victorian behemoth—not because they wanted such a colossal structure, but because it was the only house they could afford. It was cheap. In those days, no one wanted a place that big. I laugh at that today when I see the monster structures going up around us all the time. But back then, my parents and almost everyone their age had grown up in the city, lots of people packed into a few rooms or in shanties in Pennsylvania coal-mining towns. The thought of occupying a virtual castle was incomprehensible...and pointless.

The house was a child's dream. It was built on a standard fifty-foot lot that was at least a hundred feet deep. An empty lot of the same size was next to the house—part of the deal when my parents bought the house.

Exactly when the house was built is unclear except that it started out as a small one-story A-frame farmhouse dating to circa 1840. Later, a larger portion was added consisting of a second floor with several Victorian-style gables. At some point, the upper portion of the house—the gables and roof and all—had caught fire. Yet, miraculously, the fire had been extinguished, though the Victorian beauty of it was covered over with a new A-frame roof rather than restore it to the original motif.

Without question, the most exciting part of the house for a couple of small kids was a strange architectural feature that had been built into the original farmhouse. What once had probably been the tight living quarters of the austere small house had since become a massive and gorgeous foyer in the new house, complete with a large, curved staircase that rose elegantly to the second floor with a mahogany railing perfect for sliding down at break-neck speed, landing dubiously on one's feet far below.

The house had large screened-in porches that extended from the front all the way around one side on the first and second floors. The porch on the second floor connected to two of the bedrooms and served as a sleeping porch on the hot summer nights before the days of air conditioning.

The foyer also had a coat closet like any good foyer would have. However, in the back of it was a small secret door, no more than four feet high and two feet wide, which opened to a narrow set of stairs that descended into the basement. But not just into the basement, it ended at a three-foot-high stage in a room that had an old, tarnished hardwood floor and hardwood slats perfectly fitted halfway up the walls.

What the room was for—the secret staircase, the stage, the once beautiful paneling on the floor and walls—was anyone's guess. Many suggestions have been put forth. Since it was the basement of the original farmhouse before it had been expanded into its current size, it was proposed that the room had been part of the Underground Railroad where escaping slaves could wait out the day before starting their journey north again in the dark of night. In fact, a few miles away in the town of Fullersburg stands the Grau Mill, a three-story stone gristmill on the banks of Salt Creek that is documented to have been a link in the Underground Railroad.

Some have suggested that the stage had been used for

vaudeville acts and other theatrical events at the turn of the century. The local gentry would show up in carriages, proceed to a seat in the elegantly paneled basement room, and be entertained on the stage. Actors would enter and leave from the hidden staircase.

A scenario like that was feasible given that a few blocks away on Sixth Avenue other large Victorian houses had opulent third floors that were once used as elegant ballrooms. A few of them still have gilded chandeliers dating to the 1920s. One can image the carriages and Model-T Fords pulling up with couples dressed-to-the-nines—women in flowing gowns or flappers and men in tuxedoes—all set for a wild evening of champagne and dance.

Everything about living on Stone Avenue became an adventure and almost all of our time was spent out of doors, summer and winter, usually seeing how much we could get away with, or merely seeing if it were possible to test the laws of nature—gravity, let's say—in one way or another. Now it's not to say all of what we did had a good outcome, though rarely was it disastrous. But often, our young untrammeled minds led us deep into the weeds of curiosity.

I remember climbing on the roof of the garage and jumping off holding dearly onto an umbrella to see if I could float to the ground. Hey, it worked in the cartoons. I spent one afternoon doing this until the umbrella finally gave out from being turned inside out to the point where it would no longer fold up.

I don't remember where my mother was during all of this, but it was about the time my sister Patti was born. My mother seemed happy to spend most of her time inside with Patti rather than hopelessly tailing us around. And anyway, kids always played with their siblings and friends, *not* with their parents. Our parents never expected otherwise. They, themselves, had grown up independent of their parents, too. Why do anything different now?

There were a few missteps on my part, however. One was on my birthday when I was five years old. We had the usual party with a handful of neighborhood kids. The afternoon evolved into a game of cowboys and Indians. As I raced through the house chasing one of the kids who was barely two steps in front of me, he slammed a French door. My gun, my hand, my whole arm tore through the glass, and the glass tore through my arm. To this day, I have a line of scars that runs the length of my arm from my wrist to above my elbow. It looks ominously like I had tried to slice open my wrist, my whole arm in fact, from top to bottom.

The yard and the side lot made a perfect place for creating a small personal zoo. We had all the usual suspects—cats and dogs—but there were two other creatures I remember most. One was a lovely painted turtle that we had acquired at a nearby stream, a place my father loved to visit. The turtle was beautiful, about six inches across with a lovely colored shell. We brought it home (something I would never do today) and built a large sandbox with a small pond and rocks.

This majestic creature acquired the name Fred Astaire. I'm not sure who came up with the name, but it certainly was about as odd a name as could be for an animal that could make it from zero to sixty in about four years. Despite it all, Fred Astaire seemed to like his new environs and he spent the summer with us until early in the fall when we returned him to his original habitat.

We also had a large white rabbit that we named Weatherbird—another name I cannot document the origins of. Weatherbird hopped lazily around the yard at will all day, never leaving the property. At night, he was put in a hutch to keep him safe from an occasional marauding dog or cayote.

The house next to us was another grand adventure. It belonged to the Hutcheson's but had been vacant for years, having been tied up in the throes of a long divorce. It was another super-sized three-story Victorian mansion made of stone, this time with all the original gables and a stone foundation and a network of rooms deep underground—almost an Italian monastery.

We entered the house at will. I don't remember how, possibly via an open window or unlocked back door. Regardless, we spent countless hours with friends playing hide-

and-seek throughout the three stories. I remember the basement especially. One dark and eerie room after another separated by three-foot wide stone walls. Two of the rooms had been connected by a hand-hewn passage through the stone foundation, making the whole affair a virtual dungeon. Entire afternoons were spent in the house racing from one creepy room to the next.

3

ST. FRANCIS XAVIER, CHRISTMAS PAGEANT, AND ONE WEIRD SHEEP

All the Catholic neighborhoods were assigned to specific parishes. We were in the St. Francis Xavier Parish, which included a K-8 grammar school taught by the Sisters of St. Joseph. The school had a large playground next to the church that had been built in a classic basilica style in the footprint of the cross. The school was seven blocks from where we lived on Stone Avenue.

I had just started kindergarten, and Roy was in first grade. We took the school bus the seven blocks to St. Francis Xavier School. No need for parents to drive us there when a school bus would do just fine—or so it seemed. But the last thing Roy and I wanted was to sit on a dumpy bus when we could walk to school, have fun on the way, and get there about when the bus arrived, often sooner.

However, to make it even more exciting, we had to cross the Burlington railroad tracks on the way. A commuter line that sent trains barreling into Chicago at full-throttle every couple of minutes.

Well, we had a better idea. All we had to do was get near the corner where the bus was to pick us up, hide behind one of the large elm trees, wait for the bus to leave, and *voilà*, off merrily to school.

Our plan worked perfectly, for a while. Apparently one of the neighbors saw us lurking behind a tree and reported us to my mother. The next day on his way to work, my father tracked us down the block and witnessed our not-so-subtle escape. Shall I say that was the end of our trips to and from school on our own.

About the time I was in the first grade, the school was planning its annual Christmas pageant—the timeless story of Christ lying in the manger as everyone, the three wise men and all the rest, came to see and worship the Child King. Everyone in the first grade was given a part, from Christ himself, and Mary, and Joseph, and the wise men, right on down to the sheep.

As I remember, we had one or two rehearsals and then we were told what to wear. Not having secured a part as someone important. Well, not having been granted a big part, I ended up as a one of six or seven lowly sheep. That meant dressing neck-to-toe in white pajamas—those hideous things with a flap in the back and booties on the feet.

So, after one of the rehearsals, instructions were explicitly given about how to dress on the evening of the big event. The main characters, Mary, Joseph, the Maji, the others, were told to wear red lipstick. It would enhance their parts in the pageant by letting the audience see them speaking. One problem, however, I thought this meant all of us, everyone on stage right down to the sheep, were to wear red lipstick.

When I got home, I told my mother I was one of the sheep and said I needed to wear red lipstick.

"No, Johnnie, that isn't for you," she said. "It's for the kids with the speaking parts…so the audience can see who is talking. It's not for the sheep."

Of course, out of my inherent stubbornness, I argued that it was for *everyone*…yes, sheep and all.

My mother tried again, several times in fact, to explain why people were to wear lipstick and why sheep, who were not talking—well not in English, presumably—did not need to wear lipstick.

I held my ground.

She could tell she was losing the battle.

On the night of the pageant, she took me to the auditorium dressed in my cotton white pajamas and, you guessed it, wearing bright, bright red lipstick.

I was the only sheep on the stage with deep red lips of a shade that would have made Lucille Ball proud! Should have listened to my mother! It drew more than a few laughs, as I recall, including many from the audience who covered their faces with their hands and pointed to me as I knelt right there in the pack with all the rest of the 'normal' sheep.

I have always valued how, throughout my life, my

mother let me learn from my mistakes, and this was one of the best examples of it. I think I learned more from that than from pure logic. When we got home, she could tell I was more than a little embarrassed by the whole episode, though neither of us brought it up.

It was just one of the many parts of my early years as a Catholic that made little sense to me. For example, I was probably in second grade before I figured out that the first line of the Hail Mary was not, "Hail Mary, full of grace, the Lord is wiggly…". Wiggly? The Lord is wiggly? Of course, the correct line is "Hail Mary, full of grace, the Lord is with thee…" *Augh!*

So, life on Stone Avenue went predictably on, which included my eternal fascination with trains, my perpetual nemesis from as far back as I can remember. A short while later, and I don't recall exactly what led to it, on a Saturday I think, I was down along the Burlington tracks by myself near Stone Avenue Station. Roy may have been with me, but I don't remember. I was no more than five or six. Unknown to me, my mother was sitting under a hair dryer in a beauty salon looking out a window on Hillgrove Avenue that faced the Burlington line.

A string of railroad boxcars was parked on one of the sidetracks. Of course, I climbed the ladder that goes up the side of the boxcar near the wheel, which probably came up to about my shoulders, and then I zipped across the boxcars, leaping three feet to the next car, and the next one, and on and on, and then turned and came back. It was a gas; I was in heaven. I was on an actual railroad train!

Looking out the window of the beauty parlor, the woman next to my mother suddenly blurted, "Oh, my god! Look at that *little* boy hopping across the top of those *boxcars*!"

"Oh, that's terrible," my mother replied. She looked closer. "*What? Oh, no! That's Johnnie!*"

I scampered gleefully along, too delighted to know that I had been caught in the act.

Well, that was it. That did it. When my mother got home, she told my father, "We're moving to the other side of the tracks, Roy. Right away!"

I had two strikes against me. One while trying to evade the school bus with my brother and crossing the Burlington route in the process, and now hopping on the tops of boxcars. There would be no third strike for me—I was already out.

And move we did, this time to another grand house at 94 Malden Avenue north of the train tracks. By now, I had three siblings and another on the way. The total so far was my brother Roy, a year older than me, Patti, three years younger than me, and Mary Beth (MB), six years younger than me. Kurt, born four years later, would be eleven years younger than me.

The new house accommodated us very well. It was a three-story affair with a large basement that had six rooms, consisting of two small rooms with shelves for storage of canned good, and a room with an oil-burning furnace that had replaced the original coal furnace. The room had a small metal door to the outside through which coal had once been poured down a chute into a bin next to the old furnace.

There were three additional large rooms—one big enough for a ping-pong table with plenty of room to spare, a large rather generic room where the washer and dryer were, and a bulkhead at the far end of the room.

All of the three houses we lived in in La Grange had bulkheads, something you don't see in the south, largely because houses don't have basements. There was a wonderful workshop with a solid wooden bench and shelves, a large vice, and a high street-level window that let in just enough light to make the room feel airy and spacious.

The first floor had five rooms: a front sunroom surrounded by windows, a living room, a dining room, a big kitchen, and a dinette large enough for a table that could seat all seven of us.

Four rooms filled the second floor: a master bedroom, two smaller bedrooms, and a second sunroom at the back of the house, which served as a fourth bedroom.

The third floor was accessed by a set of stairs on the second floor. In one sense it was the largest room in the house because it extended the length of the entire house. My father paneled the room and converted it into a bedroom for myself and Roy. In all, the house had six bedrooms. The total room tally was seventeen. As was the case with the house on Stone Avenue, this one was a magnificent place.

The house had an elegant design that closely resembled one of several Frank Lloyd Wright homes in La Grange, though it clearly was not one, given that a nearly identical house had been built next to ours. Whoever built it apparently liked it so much they decided to put up a similar one, something I am sure Frank Lloyd Wright would never have done.

Chicago has always been a city of immigrants. In the mid-fifties, La Grange consisted mostly of families who had moved to the west side from neighborhoods closer to the city. This gave La Grange a rich ethnic mix of Irish, Italian, and Slavic groups of all sorts—Poles, Czechs, Bohemians, and plenty of Germans. The dinner tables at the houses reflected the cuisines of those groups on any day of the week. Since it was a time when few houses had air conditioning, windows were open spring, summer, and fall. All afternoon you could smell the delicious ethnic foods simmering in the kitchens as we played in the front yards and out in the street, drooling like one of Pavlov's dogs the whole while.

My mother was a spectacular cook who loved being in

the kitchen. Every day was an adventure for her and every day we were her test kitchen subjects, and what a treat it was! There, she composed her simple but wonderfully delicious meals.

Much of it consisted of traditional foods from Central and Eastern Europe, the food my father especially liked and which we all carried throughout our lives with great fondness: Bohemian roast duck with sauerkraut cooked with onion and apples and served with knedliki bread dumplings. Or kielbasa with pierogi, Polish potato dumplings, as well as my father's beloved liver dumpling soup, of course. But my mother also had a wide repertoire of Italian recipes that she had acquired from our neighbors.

We ate well every night, though rarely did we have a chance for seconds or thirds at the dinner table, food being as expensive as it was back then. And rarely was the menu heavy with meat or fatty foods.

I have always been lean and I remember at St. Francis in the second grade being repeatedly called up front to the desk of Sister Mildred (who scared the crap out of me) and being asked what I had for breakfast, or for dinner the night before, as she poked her long bony finger repeatedly into my ribs. To this day, I have no idea why I had been singled out for that embarrassing salutiferous ritual. True, I certainly was not the meatiest kid in the room, but I didn't think of myself as the skinniest either.

It is not with great fondness that I recall my days at St. Francis. Sitting from eight in the morning until recess at ten-thirty could be excruciating for a seven-year-old in Sister Mildred's class because she, and she alone, decided who could go to the bathroom. It was not unusual to hear, "No…go at recess!" Which too often meant a wet pair of pants or a wet skirt for a student.

Worse yet, I have a vivid memory of a time when Sister Mildred ridiculed a small rather chubby girl in the class. She had her stand up and for a good twenty minutes joked about her for being so plump. The class all laughed and the girl herself even did—laughed so hard that tears began to roll down her cheeks. I wasn't fooled. I knew they were tears of humiliation. I have never been able to understand how a Catholic nun could direct such animus at a child.

Were all the nuns like that? Of course not. But isn't it interesting how they are the ones we remember most?

4

LITTLE LEAGUE, ICE SKATING, HALLOWEEN, AND BLACKHAWKS GAMES

My preteen years were plenty weird compared to those of kids today. Halloween was strictly an all-kids event. Costumes consisted of something as simple as pinning a towel onto my jacket and going as Superman or cutting two holes in an old sheet and going as a ghost.

Whole packs of us would parade up and down the streets together, no parents, just us. I would bring a brown paper shopping bag, the kind with handles on it, to carry the loot I collected while trick-or-treating. When it got too full I would buzz home, dump everything on the table, and race out to continue with the rest of the crowd.

But definitely the stupidest thing we did happened during the hot months in the summer when the mosquitoes were bad. Trucks drove down one street after another spraying a gigantic dense fog of insecticide. When it came by our house we would charge out and run through the fog, back and forth across it. We would do this for several blocks and then come home almost dripping with the stuff. My mother took one look and sent us to the bathroom for a very long shower.

I don't know what the chemical composition of the insecticide was, but one thing you can be sure of, it was not intended to be sprayed on people. Now, in actuality, it was not that my mother had no concern for our personal health and well-being. It was just that in the 1950s very little was understood about the risks of chemicals in our lives; new ones were coming out almost daily. Consider that in 1948 the Nobel Prize in Physiology or Medicine had been awarded to Paul Hermann Müller for his discovery of DDT—a chemical that is illegal in nearly every country today.

When we would go to Dr. Luke's office, our family physician, for a minor medical issue, he always had an ashtray on the counter in the exam rooms, frequently with a cigarette burning that he would stop and take a puff from. It was typical for doctors back then to recommend that patients, usually women, take up smoking. "It will help relax your nerves," they would say.

We spent almost every free moment outdoors—winter, summer, spring, and fall—playing with our friends. One summer a bunch of us tried out for Little League. We all made it onto a team. Mine was sponsored by one of the banks in La Grange. Finally, the day came for us to pick up our uniforms. The name of the bank was on the front. On the back was a number…mine turned out to be number one. Not the number I would have chosen but at least I had made it on a team. Then the big blow came. I learned that the numbers had been put on the uniforms based on the size of it. There it was, I had the smallest number because I had the smallest uniform because I was the smallest player on the team. I was devastated.

When I got home, I told my mother about this. In her wonderfully empathetic way she said, "No, Johnnie, that's not what it means. They gave you that number because you're the best player on the team…the number one player." It was a good attempt, but I knew the real reason.

Little League was fun. But, wow, was it ever different then than now. On Saturdays when we had our games, we rode our bikes to the park. No parents, just us. In fact, my father never came to any of my games. Was I bothered? Not in the least. Little League was for kids, not for parents. We had no problem with that. Nor did our parents, apparently.

I was a terrible baseball player. The entire season, I never got a single hit. Not one! In fact, I struck out almost every time at bat. The team stuck me in right field, figuring most kids our age couldn't knock a ball that far out, at least not in the air. And it was basically true. The few times it happened, however, there I was with my baseball mitt perched high overhead only to drop every ball that came to me, or more often than not, to see it thump down five or six feet to my left or right. Oh well, I never aspired for a career in big league baseball, anyway.

One day, Billy, a friend of mine, said, "John, guess what? Sherm Lollar lives two doors down from us on Brewster."

My eyes popped out. "Sherm...Lollar?" I said. "You mean Sherm Lollar the catcher for the Chicago White Sox?"

Sherm Lollar was no slacker when it came to baseball. He played eighteen years in major league baseball with several teams including eleven of them with the White Sox, and had been selected as an American League All-Star seven times.

"Yeah...him," Billy said.

Brewster was a short unimpressive street a few blocks north of Ogden Avenue.

It turned out that during the baseball season, Sherm Lollar lived on Brewster with his family—a plain, simple bungalow with a big front porch, great for spending lazy afternoons sipping lemonade, and on days when the Sox weren't playing, that was exactly what Sherm did.

In the 1950s a typical baseball player made about as much as an average workman's wage. My father, who didn't have a large income by any stretch, may well have made more than most big-league players. In fact, Sherm didn't own the place he was staying in. He merely rented it for the summer baseball season and then went down to Florida where he rented another place for the off-season.

So, Billy said, "C'mon, let's go to Sherm's house and see if he's sitting on the porch. We can pitch balls to him."

"You're kidding!"

"No, he's a real cool guy. Get your mitt."

We rode our bikes over to Brewster and, sure enough, there was Sherm on the porch just as Billy had predicted. We parked our bikes at Billy's and walked two doors down to the Lollar place.

"Hey, Mr. Lollar," Billy piped. "Can we pitch some balls to you?"

"Hell yes," Sherm replied with a broad grin. He got up and went into the house and came out to the front lawn with his big round catcher's mitt.

He crouched down and pretended to give a sign. Billy leaned forward, watched the sign that Sherm flashed with the fingers of his right hand between his legs. Billy stood up, shoulders cranked back, did a wind up and winged his best fast ball, which in fact sort of floated through the air to Sherm. He pulled it from his mitt and tossed it back for another delivery. We went back and forth like that—Billy, then me, then Billy, then me. For several hours a couple days a week all summer, we pitched and Sherm snagged our wild 'fast' balls out of the air…or off the ground.

It's hard today to actually put this in perspective. Hard

to imagine very many players from any major league baseball team doing this with neighborhood kids today. Baseball players—like all professional athletes—are near deities who live in an alternate universe in mansions with high fences that are much like the moats on medieval castles.

In the summer we were outside on the street playing baseball all day. Our street had a mob of kids, mostly all within a couple of years of each other—all boomer kids. Tallying up the list today I can remember something like twenty-seven from just a handful of houses up and down the block. The girls played hopscotch or jumped rope. The boys (and some of the girls, too) played baseball in the street. We marked home plate and second base with a chalk X in the street. First and third were marked with a stone or whatever was handy.

One evening Roy and I decided to make a fancy addition to the street baseball diamond. We went to a construction site down on the corner where a new house was being built and found a piece of scrap wood. Nice and square, twelve inches or so on each side, and a good inch thick. It would was perfect. All we needed to do was to cut diagonal pieces from two corners and we would have a beautiful home plate.

It didn't go so well. We took the piece of wood to the basement workshop in our house and marked exactly where we wanted the corner cuts. Roy climbed on the work bench and knelt on the wood. His weight was mostly enough to keep the wood from moving, but I held it on the front to help steady it. I grabbed the wood with all my might while Roy took hefty slices with a sharp carpenter's crosscut saw. Up-down, up-down, up-down. Again and again. It was going great. But, unfortunately, just as he leaned into a fierce downward swipe, the index finger of my left hand was perfectly placed under the wood in the path of the blade. Slam, crunch. In one fell swoop the tip of my finger was on the floor.

I screamed and ran upstairs holding my finger, gushing blood. My parents took one look, wrapped my hand in a towel, and we sped off the ER at the local hospital. To this day, my finger has a perfect angle where the blade flew across it and it's about a quarter inch shorter than my other index finger. I have often wondered if I am the only person to lose a fingertip from a hand saw.

Winter weekends were spent at Gilbert Park five blocks from where we lived. As soon as temperatures went below freezing, the park system flooded a large patch of the park. It was open from nine in the morning until nine at night, complete with lights to permit skating after the sun went down.

I knew how to skate from the time I was four, when my father took us in the winter afternoons to Salt Creek that flowed through nearby Fullersburg next to the old Grau

Mill.

But it was at Gilbert Park that I really learned to skate. I can remember being at the park from early in the morning until it closed, sometimes racing home for a quick sandwich and then returning to skate, or maybe eat a sandwich I had brought in the morning.

The park had a warming house so on the hideously cold Chicago days one could skate for hours with a couple of visits to the warming house. By the time I was eight years old, I was doing hockey stops in both directions, skating backwards, and doing crossovers in both directions.

A couple of times every season, the park would hold races. Ice skates come in three version: figure skates, hockey skates, and racer skates. The three stars for our age group were Tim Reilly, Johnnie Lockrem, and John Torrey, all three of whom soared across the ice on racer skates.

Everyone I grew up with was a rabid Chicago Blackhawks fan, which at that time played at the Chicago Stadium, an old arena built in 1929. Off and on throughout the winter, a bunch of us would take the Burlington commuter train to the stadium for a Hawks night game.

I would say, "Mom, everyone is going to a Hawks game. Can I go?"

"Who is everyone?" she would ask.

I would rattle off a string of names, all kids my age, not a single adult.

She would think it over for a second, then say, "Ooh…I suppose. How are you getting there?"

"Taking the train."

I'd give a quick call to a friend and tell him I was set to go. We would get on the Burlington at the Stone Avenue Station or the La Grange Road Station, take the train to Western Avenue, and hoof it the rest of the way to the Stadium. The stadium, old as it was, continued to be used until the current stadium on West Madison Street (the Madhouse on Madison) was built in 1995.

We would buy tickets for the cheapest seats at the stadium, the nose-bleed seats in the top tier that would actually shake slightly when the stadium got too full or when icy winds blew up outside. And there was no guarantee that one of the seats might not be directly behind—and I mean directly behind—a huge twelve-by-twelve-inch I-beam, which occasionally happened to one of us. Fortunately, we usually managed to move down the row away from the beam. It was grand to be there with just our friends and, after buying a ticket, we all had just enough money for a hot dog and a soda.

When the game was over, we'd retrace our steps, climb on the Burlington, and ride back to La Grange. Our parents were not seated at home waiting with bated breath for us to arrive. Somehow, they knew and believed all would be well.

Regardless, virtually everything described in this

chapter—little league, ice skating at the park in winter, riding the train downtown to Chicago Blackhawk games, Halloween trick-or-treating, and yes even running through a cloud of mosquito insecticide—we did on our own, totally without parents at our sides for better or for worse.

Some years later when I was in my early twenties, we would go after Blackhawks games to The Sportsman's Lounge in Cicero on the near west side of Chicago. It was a simple local tavern that had a plain wooden bar and a half dozen oilcloth tables. We would never have known about it except that my sister Patti had a friend, Diane Bogdan, whose family had owned the bar for years.

About forty-five minutes after the Hawks games, Bobby Hull, Stan Mikita, and Tony Esposito would come strolling into the bar with their wives—all dressed-to-kill in suede or leather or cashmere coats with fur collars. They would pull up a stool at the bar and order drinks.

When I think about this today, the most amazing thing is that hardly anyone but the local patrons of the bar and the Bogdan's who owned it knew that three of the greatest hockey players of all times would stop in for a couple hours of drinking. Today, there would be a mob of people outside for autographs.

We would sit at one of the tables and drink beer, ecstatically waiting for them to come in. Since this was before social media, there was no mechanism for the word of their pending arrival to spread. I'm not sure the people having a beer and a shot at the bars across the street or down the block even knew what was taking place a short distance away.

Bobby Hull, Stan Mikita, and Tony (Tony O) Esposito each played the better part of their long careers with the Blackhawks, and each was famous in one way or another. Bobby Hull had unmatched skill with the puck and one of the hardest slapshots ever recorded in the league. Both Bobby Hull and Stan Mikita each scored more than five hundred career goals.

Though they did not invent the slapshot, they were the first to use hockey sticks with curved blades. Back then, sticks were made of wood and had straight blades. The story goes that Stan Mikita earned the reputation as the father of the curved blade when the tip of his stick cracked one day; he discovered that he could control and lift the puck better. This led Bobby and Stan to soak their sticks in water and wedge them under a doorjamb to create a bend in the blade. The rest is history. Today, no one plays with a straight blade.

Tony O's claim to fame is equally legendary for his introduction of the butterfly style of net minding, a style that today is used by one hundred percent of all goalies. Prior to that, goal tending was done standing straight up.

What an enormous thrill it was to watch this trinity of great players come into a simple bar on the west side of

Chicago on a winter night when temperatures outside dipped into the twenties or teens. Surely, they could have gone to some upscale establishment given that Chicago is a city of taverns and bars—somewhere in the order of ten thousand in all—of every imaginable style and type.

5

ALTAR BOY AND FATHER O'GARA

Along about the time I was in the fourth grade I became an altar boy at St. Francis Xavier Church. La Grange had strong Catholic underpinnings, so much so that every morning during the week there were daily masses at six, six-thirty, seven, seven-thirty, and eight o'clock. The first four masses were low masses; the eight o'clock mass was a high mass. Sunday masses seemed to go on all day. There was one at seven, eight, nine, ten-fifteen, eleven-fifteen, and twelve-fifteen.

The church and school were on the south side of Ogden Avenue. Immediately across Ogden on the north side was a public elementary school, one of many public schools in the area. I remember the nuns at St. Francis telling us we were *not* to go across Ogden unless we had a very good reason because that's where the "Protestant school" was. Yes, the "Protestant school" as they called it, not the public school. Looking back at it, you'd think we were living in Belfast. Or as if being near the Protestant school would screw up our thinking and we would suddenly become like Martin Luther and renounce Catholicism.

Altar boys were assigned to one of the scheduled mass

times for a couple of weeks. My routine—and that of most of the other altar boys in my class—was to pedal my bike to the church, serve as an altar boy, pedal quickly home, have breakfast, and pedal back to school.

If I had been assigned the six o'clock mass, I vividly remember riding the eight blooks to the church in total darkness before the sun had come up. Of all my altar boy memories, the one I remember most was when, after finishing serving mass with Father O'Gara he told me to go over to Hank's, a tiny store just across Ogden Avenue (on the Protestant side of the street) that offered a very simple fare of milk, a few canned goods, bread—the essentials. Hank and his family lived in a house next to the store.

Father O'Gara said to go to Hank's and get a newspaper and bring it to the rectory.

I climbed out of my cassock and went out and jumped on my bike and headed over to Hank's, barely a block away. When I got there, Hank's hadn't opened yet. The newspapers were sitting on the steps wrapped tightly in wire.

I thought, "Oh, geez, now what?" Of all the priests to report back to, Father O'Gara was on the top of the list for making the knees of an eight-year-old knock loud enough to wake up the neighbors.

I tore back to the rectory and went into the kitchen where Father O'Gara was finishing breakfast.

"Hank's isn't open yet," I said. "The papers are on the

porch, but they're tied in wire."

"Well, *break* it!" Father O'Gara growled.

I stood there with my mouth agape. Let's figure this out, I thought. Father O'Gara, a Catholic priest, wants me to steal a newspaper.

"Break the wire and get a paper," he repeated.

I went out, climbed on my bike, pedaled like hell over to Hank's again, fearing the wrath of Hank if he were to catch me in the act of ripping open his papers.

Now, how was I going to break the wire? Of course, Pat (Packy) Burns, a classmate, lived a couple of three doors down from Hank's.

Next stop, Packy's house to explain my predicament. With wire cutters in hand, I returned to the crime scene and snapped the wire, then pumped my way back to the rectory in record time.

I handed Father O'Gara the paper.

"I'll go over to Hank's this afternoon and square up with him about the paper," he calmly said.

Oh, thank you, I thought. Thank you. Absolution…yes!

But not all the priests were as terrorizing as Father O'Gara. Father McGlinn was a young priest whose first assignment was St. Francis Parish. He drove a two-tone grey and black 1957 Chevrolet and periodically he would come by in the evenings to the houses of some of the altar boys.

"Mom, it's Father McGlinn," we'd cry. "He wants to know if we can go to McDonalds with him!"

In the late 50s, La Grange had one of the first McDonalds restaurants. We'd race out to the car. Father McGlinn would make several more stops and soon the front and back seats were full. As we headed across town, he would show us how he could drive the car with his knees. No hands, just knees. Of course, we all loved it. When I got home, I told my mother about this. All she did was shake her head as I recall.

The McDonalds was strictly a drive-up fast-food restaurant that initially had carhops. We would place our order for a hamburger, fries, and a Coke. That's about all they sold. We'd eat the burgers and fries in the car and head back across town usually with our drinks, and with Father McGlinn occasionally driving with his knees again. Somewhere along the way he'd say, "Straws are for girls!" and he would flip his straw out the window of the car, which was immediately followed by a chorus of "Straws are for girls!" A half dozen straws would go flying out the windows all at once. This clearly was well before the days of women's liberation.

Shortly after that, Father McGlinn was transferred to a Spanish-speaking parish in Chicago and later requested to work in Central America, which the diocese agreed to.

6

WORKING AT MY FATHER'S RESTAURANT AND MY INTRODUCTION TO THE MOB

My father quit his job and bought a restaurant, figuring he would have a better chance of making a living if he had total control of the decisions. It was located on the South Side of Chicago at 111th Street and Harlem Avenue. The restaurant sold just about everything you could imagine, hot dogs, hamburgers, tamales, chili, ice cream cones, sundaes, banana splits, milkshakes, soft drinks.

It was a grueling undertaking by my father because it opened in the morning at nine and went straight through until around ten at night. Seven days a week. He worked it almost entirely by himself; now and then one part-time employee, maybe, but mostly just him.

In the summer and occasionally on weekends I worked at the restaurant, as did Roy now and then. I'm not sure how much money my father made on those days given that it became a near non-stop smorgasbord event for me. But it was fun being there and I liked every minute of it.

Eventually, my father started selling Chicago Italian

beef sandwiches. My mother would roast a large lean piece of beef and my father would slice it into thin strips with a meat slicer and then soak it in a deliciously spiced broth until it was ready for sandwiches. If you've ever had a Chicago Italian beef sandwich, you will know what I am talking about. If you haven't, life is not complete until you've tried one.

Apparently, the sandwich was invented by Italian immigrants who worked in the stockyards. They would bring home the cheap cuts of meat and turn them into Italian Beef sandwiches just like they're made today. Customarily, they're served on a hoagie roll with cooked green peppers, hot or sweet, and soaked with the broth, then wrapped in foil, and handed to the customer.

Never ever, ever, ever is it served with cheese on it! It's not cheesesteak. I've heard at least one Chicagoan say, "If yer gonna put cheese on a Chicago beef sandwich, den ya might as well put ketchup on da hot dog" (also sacrilegious in Chicago). To Chicagoans, ketchup on hot dogs would be like slapping mustard on Bar-B-Que to a Southerner.

The restaurant had a window to order from, but it also had indoor seating at a small counter—eight or ten low, twirly, diner-style stools in front of a low counter. A jukebox stood in the corner with all the popular 1950s records. Elvis, Buddy Holly, Frankie Avalon, Ricky Nelson, Dion.

However, if there ever was a moment that was forever

carved into my memory, it was one day when a man came into the restaurant, shook my father's hand, took a key from his pocket, and opened the jukebox. He pulled a few 45 records out and put a few new ones in and asked my father if there were any records that he would like replaced. My father shrugged and nonchalantly shook his head.

The man then removed the container inside the jukebox where the nickels, dimes, and quarters were, brought it to the counter, and spread the coins in a low pile. I watched unable to figure out what was going on as he took his hand and split the pile into two halves. One half for my father. One half for the man. He looked across the counter at my father and pointed to the two piles. "Fair?" he asked.

My father nodded.

The man gathered one of the piles and slid the coins into a cloth bag and tied it shut. I do remember that the pile my father got was ever so slightly bigger than the one the man took. Not much but noticeably so.

They shook hands again and the man left.

I was shocked, dismayed. I had no idea what was going on. Finally, I asked my father, "Who was that guy?"

"He owns the jukebox," my father said as he returned to the grill full of simmering hamburgers. "He owns the jukebox, so he gets half the money that's in it."

"Well, why don't you just get your own jukebox, and then you can keep all the money?"

My father stopped cooking. He set the spatula down and looked at me, and in the most serious voice, said, "If I did that, Johnnie, this place would be burned to the ground when I came here tomorrow."

In time I learned that this was merely part of the tight grip the mob has had on Chicago for an eternity. Every jukebox, thousands of them throughout the city, were owned by the mob. Think of it. Without an ounce of competition, they grossed tens of thousands of dollars by getting half of all the nickels, dimes, and quarters dropped into jukeboxes. They brought you the jukebox and took it away if you didn't want it. They even replaced the one in my father's restaurant at no charge when it totaled-out and quit playing one day.

But it wasn't just the jukeboxes. The mob also had complete control over restaurant linen. You could not send out napkins, tablecloths, or aprons to your local cleaner. Nor so with the cloth hand towels in the rest rooms. In the 1950s pre-paper towel time, every restaurant, every bar in the city had linen towels.

And then to complete the trifecta, the mob made and supplied all the Italian sausage in the city of Chicago. Don't dare to make your own or buy it from another supplier. If there was a scintilla of justification for this, it was that—in my rather heavily biased opinion—the Italian sausage used on the pizzas and in the Italian food in Chicago is unmatched anywhere in the US. For better or for worse, the mob got that one right.

As you might expect, the mob in Chicago played a far more pernicious game than jukeboxes, linen, and sausage. They had total control over most of the gambling in the city. I knew this all too well from Tommy Donahue, a kid I grew up with. His father owned a busy gas station on the corner of 47th Street and Gilbert Avenue. He had several tow trucks, an ambulance, and a large and beautiful house on Seventh Avenue in La Grange. *And*, he had a big addiction to gambling. One night while in a game in the back room of a bar he got in over his head. Worse, these were not people you told you would square with later. This he knew, so he set the deed for his house, his gas station, and all his trucks on the table to cover his debt, undoubtedly figuring he would be able to come up with the cash to clean the slate of his bad night of poker.

Two days later on a rainy night while returning from Indiana with a casket to deliver to a funeral home in La Grange, his ambulance slid off the road and hit a guard rail. He survived the crash but died a couple hours later from a ruptured spleen.

Barely a day after, two men showed up with a handful of deeds that they displayed to Mrs. Donahue. The family lost everything. Tommy's version was that his father had been run off the road. "He was too good a driver to just swerve over onto a rail. Those fuckers, those bastards from the mob, they ran him off the road because they wanted to clean him out. And they did!"

The family moved into a shitty cramped apartment above the *La Grange Lanes*, a large bowling alley in the center of town. Tommy, still in his early teens, spent most of his time hanging out at the bowling alley. Ironically, not only did he become a crackerjack bowler but he, too, developed a gambling addiction, this time as a bowling hustler.

By the time he was eighteen, he was hustling in bowling alleys throughout the city. I would occasionally go with him on his expensive escapades. Most of the big-time hustlers knew each other. It was a tightknit clique. They knew who was good and who was just fair.

The game was always the same. Either five for five, or five for a thousand, as they called it: five games for five hundred dollars, or five games for a thousand dollars. The first one to win five games, won it all. It was a tense, high stakes proposition full of psychological warfare as they rolled balls down the alley in total silence one after another, and it never ended with just one set. The loser always demanded a double-or-nothing rematch to recover the loss, which could go on until they either came back and won, or they threw in the towel and paid up. A hell of a lot of money changed hands. But as with poker, you damn well had better be ready if you lost, which usually meant toting the deed for a new very classy, very expensive car. Hustlers were flashy as hell, and they flashed all the time. It was part of their bravado. When it came to this, Tommy was a pro.

Later, when I was old enough to go to a bar with my friends on a Saturday night, the next morning my father would ask where we had gone. When I told him some of the places we had hit, he would reply, saying, "You know you shouldn't go to that place. It's a mob bar."

To which I would reply, "They're all mob bars, Dad. You know that."

He knew it. Although not all the bars in Chicago were mob bars, there was a heavy dose of them that were.

A few years ago, my wife Jeanne and I were visiting my mother in Clarendon Hills, an area west of La Grange. After we spent an evening at my mother's apartment, we decided to stop and have a drink before going back to our hotel. Driving along Ogden Avenue, most of the places were closed, except for one. We parked and went inside. It was about as typical a Chicago bar as you could find. Lights down low, long bar, tables where people could sit and drink and eat. We sat at a table near the bar. Glancing over, I noticed two men, each with shiny sharkskin suits, pinky rings with diamonds so large they shot off glittering light: "rocks", as we called them back in my Chicago days.

Eventually, a guy came in dressed exactly as the two at the bar. One of the guys got up immediately and went over…big hug. They were just a few feet from us. So close that we heard one of them say, "Hey, Vinnie, Vinnie, Vinnie…where ya bin old buddy? Where ya bin? Ain't seen ya in ages."

Jeanne looked at me in amazement. She had heard about this display of mob brotherhood but had never witnessed it firsthand. I couldn't help but laugh under my breath as we sat in the dimly lit tavern with the sparkle of the diamonds from the pinky rings on the pair next to us.

7

A Paper Route, Breaking up the Boredom, Hooky, And a Very Bad Train Ride

I guess I was in the sixth grade when I decided I wanted a paper route. Tom Baer, a friend of mine, had a morning route and it seemed like great fun and a chance to make a little money.

I popped the idea on my mother. "Well...oh I suppose," she replied in her usual manner. "What's involved?"

I explained that the news agency assigned a route and then every morning bright and early they would drop the papers on the porch at three-thirty or four. I would fold them, load them into a large basket on the front of my bike, and ride up and down the street winging the papers onto the doorsteps from the sidewalk.

My mother listened intently, then took in a deep breath and again said, "Well...I suppose so. Okay."

I was ecstatic.

She added one additional caveat. "Now remember, Johnnie," she said, looking at me with very serious eyes. "This is *your* paper route, *not* mine. I am not getting up at the crack of dawn to drive you from door to door delivering papers."

"Of course," I assured her. "Of course." Anyway, the last thing I wanted was for my mother to haul me down the street on my paper route. I was capable of doing it, and even at ten years of age I had no worries about riding along the dark blocks of La Grange at five or six in the morning.

I raced off to the news agency and put in my request for a route. As it turned out, they had one that just came open and it couldn't have been a better location. It started one block behind our house and went for four more blocks.

In all, I delivered to about a hundred and sixty households, winter, summer, spring, and fall. The routine was simple. By the time I opened the front door at five-thirty, the papers were on the porch tied in tight bundles with wire (exactly like at Hank's when Father O'Gara sent me off for his morning paper theft).

Six days a week I was up long before the sun came up, preparing the papers, and delivering them to the neighborhood. It was my first true paying job. At the end of the month, I went to the news agency on Burlington Avenue across from the La Grange Road train station and picked up a brown envelope with the grand total of about thirty dollars, roughly one dollar each day. What's more, every morning there was an extra incentive in the form of a quarter (twenty-five cents) that came in an envelope with the papers, provided there had been no complaints the day before.

To me, this was funny money, something to be spent on a candy bar or an ice cream bar. Until my father learned what I was doing with it.

"What? You're spending the quarter on candy? No, no, no, no! Not any more you're not! From now on it goes into a bank for when you really need it."

How outrageous, I thought. Squandering an entire quarter each day! You have to be kidding.

But, of course, as always seemed to happen, it didn't take long for trouble to catch up to me. I don't know whether I went looking for trouble or whether it came looking for me. But however it happened, I couldn't help playing a harmless prank on one of my paper route customers—an annoying geezer who always bitched to the news agency, claiming I had screwed up somehow, had flung his paper into the bushes or some crap like that. Of course, it cost me my quarter the next morning.

So, one afternoon I was sitting in the basement with Steve, a friend from St. Francis, doing not much of anything. A few old newspapers from days and weeks gone by were spread around. One of us, no doubt me, came up with a wild idea. Why not take the geezer's morning paper tomorrow and glue an old headline on top of the real one? It was a stupid idea that only a ten-year-old might come up with. I picked out the most outrageous headline I could find (I don't remember today what it was). The next morning, I cut it out very carefully and glued it over the real headline. The man was furious, the news agency was furious, I caught holy hell for my prank.

For some reason, everything seemed to be getting evermore crazy as I pushed the limit more and more all the time.

We used to go over to Jimmy O'Connell's house after school. His father had built a great club room in the basement that had a bar and a real jukebox much like the one my father had in his restaurant, and a regulation size pool table.

Jimmy and I were knocking pool balls around the table when one of us hatched the idea to play hooky from school the next day. Every kid played hooky at some time in their life…uh, right? Of course, we had no legitimate reason to do it. We didn't have a big math assignment due, or some sort of term paper. Nothing special at all. But we would play hooky, nonetheless. We had it all planned.

Instead of going to school the next morning, we met at a park a few blocks from my house. It had lots of trees and high bushes that were perfect for hiding out in. We had nothing in particular planned, and had nothing in particular that we would do while we were there except move from bush to bush hoping not to be seen.

But, of course, we *did* get noticed. I am not sure how; I think someone in one of the houses along the park spotted us slinking along like gnomes between the bushes. In any event, when I got home at the usual time from school, my mother confronted me with a very direct question. "So, Johnnie, tell me, how was school today?" I knew I had been nabbed. All attempts to dodge the question were useless.

Unquestionably, however, the worst of my escapades was a gross scheme that was hatched with two of my friends, who shall remain nameless. I don't remember which of us came up with the plot.

La Grange in the 1950s had a large and elegant movie theater that dated back to Vaudeville days. There were tiers of seats, a stage up front that was no longer used for live performances but above which a movie screen permanently hung. Along the sides of the theater were chic box seats that provided a bird's eye view of the stage. A balcony stretched across the back with eight or ten rows of seats that jutted out above the last few rows of seats below.

The three of us went to a Saturday matinee, bought tickets, and went up to the balcony which on that day was nearly empty. We selected a location in the front row above a teenage boy and his girlfriend who were holding hands in the seats below, apparently on an afternoon movie date. I removed a can of Del Monte Creamed Corn from my jacket, opened it with a can opener, and handed it to one of my cohorts in crime. Carefully aiming it on our targets, he dumped the corn onto the two unfortunate victims below, accompanied by gurgling and gagging sounds as if getting sick to his stomach.

We dropped the empty can in the balcony and fled out the side exist.

◻

Trains of all kinds had fascinated me my entire life, even to the point of running across the top of boxcars when I was barely five years old, as described previously. In truth, that was a harmless escapade on my part given that the rail car was off on a sidetrack and not attached to an engine.

This stunt was a whole lot more dangerous.

It all started on a Saturday afternoon when, along with two of my friends, all about twelve years old, we 'found ourselves' in a big train yard on the eastern edge of La Grange. It had dozens of tracks that were used to string boxcars onto freight trains. I don't even remember what prompted us to go there.

We snooped around and then one of us climbed onto the ladder of a slow-moving train as it passed by. Wow! Cool! We rode the train hanging onto the ladder with one foot on the lower rung and then jumped off after the train had gone fifty or sixty yards down the tracks and waited for a train that was creeping along in the other direction and rode it back.

We did this for most of the afternoon. Getting on the

ladder to ride the train was incredibly challenging and, I might add, incredibly dangerous. Mind you, we were not even out of middle school. As the train passed, we needed to run along at the same speed as the train, grab a rung of the ladder, pull ourselves up onto the moving train and get a foot onto the bottom rung of the ladder.

Next time you see a boxcar on a moving train, take a close look at the design. There is no room for error. One slip and you're under the massive steel wheel of the boxcar. To make it even more dangerous, calculating the speed of the train was essential because once you've grabbed the ladder, the momentum of the moving train jerked you forward very hard—even on a very slow moving one.

But being naïve and young and stupid, we gave no thought to all the disasters that could have happened.

In fact, when we got to school on Monday we raved about our adventure at the train yard. Pretty soon we convinced a pack of our classmates to give it a try next Saturday.

The train yard was the same; trains moving along fairly slowly up and down the yard. I demonstrated the trick to hitching a ride on a boxcar. Pretty soon everyone was taking small rides on the boxcars, holding on for dear life to the ladder. To sink us deeper into the weeds of trouble, there were cabooses at the ends of trains. These were the days before cabooses had been retired from freight trains. Of course, it was impossible not to go inside a caboose and see what it was like. Two things were immediately evident: railroad flares and blasting caps that were used to signal the engineer to stop or slow down. The cap was wrapped around the rail with a lead band and exploded when the wheel of the train ran over it.

Wow, what fun!

We took a box of caps and strung the rails with them. Exactly as predicted, there was a loud blast when the wheel hit them. It was like the Fourth-of-July right there at the railroad yard.

Well, that's what did us in. Oblivious to what would come of this, we continued to ride on the boxcars and blow off blasting caps.

Suddenly, farther down the tracks, I saw men who looked very mean and pissed-off coming toward us—railroad police. We all headed in a half dozen directions, the police not far behind.

In my case, I fled into an area of cheap houses along the rail yard and climbed into a basement window well where I squeezed down and tried not to be noticed. No, it did not work. Soon, I was staring up at a very gruff looking man who was waving a big .45 caliber pistol down on me, ordering me out of the well.

We were taken to the police station where our mothers were called to come and get us. The railroad police said we had been down at the yard "flipping freights"—old railroad jargon for riding freight trains as hobos of yore used to do. To this day my mother still thinks we were turning the boxcars over, flipping them off the tracks. How you could possibly do that, I have no idea, but that's what she thought we were doing.

8

JOE COFFEE DRINKER

Back in the fifties when a major household appliance such as a washing machine or a dryer broke, it was not discarded as is often done today, put out by the curb for heavy trash. Rather, it was fixed—many times, in fact.

In La Grange there was a man who could fix anything. His name was Joe Vinicki, and everyone knew to call Joe when something was broken. He would show up in the evening wearing a pair of bibbed overalls and a plain blue shirt. He had short grey-black stubbles of hair and he bore the face of someone whose ancestors had come from some Slavic country.

Joe was the neighborhood repairman, though in fact he had a first-rate white-collar job as an engineer at Western Electric on the west side of Chicago.

My mother had heard about Joe from her friends. He had a large Catholic family with many kids. They lived in a turn-of-the-century three-story house across from St. Francis.

Joe could fix anything, assuming he would get around to it once he came over. Joe liked to talk…a lot! According to my mother, going around town fixing appliances for people was Joe's way of getting out of the house at night. It was his evening's peace and quiet.

So, Joe would show up around seven or so in the evening and of course all the usual courtesies were extended to him as for any 'house guest' back in those days.

"Want something to drink, Joe?" my mother would say.

"Oh, sure, Mary. Cup of coffee maybe."

My mother would start a percolator of fresh coffee boiling. Joe would sit at the table in the kitchen, where there was always an ashtray in those days, and pull out a pack of Camels from his overall pocket, light one up, and start chatting with my mother, who knew Joe's family well.

My father would come by on his way to reading the evening newspaper in the living room. "Hi Joe. Here to fix the washer?"

"Oh, yeah, Roy. We'll have it working again in no time."

In fact, "no time" turned out to be a hell of a long time.

Joe would sit and talk with my mother, drink coffee, smoke Camels, and the evening would wear on. It was my brother Roy who had dubbed him 'Joe Coffee Drinker.'

At dinner my mother would say, "Joe Vinicki is coming by to fix the washing machine."

And my brother would instantly say, "Huh? Joe Coffee Drinker?"

I have to say, Roy pegged that one perfectly.

And so, Joe would sit at the table smoking and putting away the better part of a whole pot of coffee (I have no idea how he managed to sleep at night).

Along about ten o'clock he'd say, "Well, okay, let me take a look at that washer of yours, Mary." He'd head into the basement.

I'd usually follow him down and watch with great curiosity. It never took long for him to figure out the problem. He'd remove the culprit, bring it to the kitchen, and say something like, "Needs a new starter. I'll have to pick one up. Won't take long. A day or two, Mary."

"Oh, Joe, more time without a washing machine?"

"Won't be too long, Mary."

In a day or two, Joe would be back. Another three hours in the kitchen with a pot of coffee and a pack of Camels. Ten minutes in the basement and he'd surface in the kitchen again.

"All done. Works like a charm, Mary."

My mother would gasp in relief. "Oh, that's great, Joe. Here, let me pay you."

Joe would hold his hand up and say, "Ah, oh no. Not now. Let's give it a couple of days to see how it's doing."

"Oh, Joe, take something now."

He never did. I don't think Joe Coffee Drinker ever took a nickel for any of his work.

9

SO YOU WANT TO BE A MISSIONARY

St. Francis was always pushing the eighth-grade boys to go into the seminary, hoping that they would someday become priests. In fact, lots of the eighth-grade class took the bait and went to Quigley High School, the diocesan school for young seminarians.

In my case it was slightly different. Tim Reilly, my best friend, had a cousin who was a Maryknoll priest. He was in the recruitment department of Maryknoll and had been assigned to Chicago. The recruiters lived in a wonderful old brownstone house in the Gold Coast region of Chicago, a few blocks from the lake north of the Loop. Tim and I took the train into the Loop to visit his cousin. Little by little, the idea of going to the Maryknoll seminary seemed much more exotic than being with the Quigley crowd.

Maryknoll, or officially The Catholic Foreign Missionary Society of America, had three junior seminaries. One, known as The Venard, named for a French missionary who had been martyred in China, was in Scranton, Pennsylvania. The second was in Mountain View, California. The third was brand new and had just finished construction in

Chesterfield, Missouri. Seminarians were assigned to the seminary based on geography. Tim and I would be going to Chesterfield.

Maryknoll was devoted to foreign mission work in Southeast Asia, Central and South America, and parts of Africa. What set Maryknoll apart from other missionary orders was its commitment to combating poverty and improving social justice as much as spirituality. They were referred to as the Marines of the Catholic Church because of how they integrated themselves into the lives of the people they served. This, however, frequently drew the wrath of the Vatican, which accused the Order of being left-leaning and communist in its orientation.

The doctrine of the Maryknoll Order seemed right to me. I had no desire to spend my life saying morning and Sunday masses, doing weddings and funerals and benedictions, and hearing confessions, as made up the life of most diocesan priests. Living in an exotic country and working with Indigenous People, sounded exhilarating.

So, off we went, Tim and I, age fourteen, to Maryknoll Seminary in Chesterfield, Missouri. The seminary was on a large stretch of bucolic land, several hundred acres of rolling hills, forests, streams, and a small lake.

We stayed at the seminary for nine months and came home for three months in the summer. We were not permitted to leave the property except for a couple of hours on

Sunday and were only allowed to have visitors for four hours one Sunday afternoon a month. Life was monastic, to say the least. We slept in dormitories, arose at six o'clock, went to chapel for meditation and morning mass, made our beds. Every minute of which was spent in strict silence.

We then went to breakfast, where we were allowed to talk for the first time. Suddenly, the volume in the refectory rose to a high level.

After breakfast, we had fifteen minutes of morning duties (short work details), then to class from nine to noon. Chapel at noon for prayers and lunch in the refectory followed by a half hour of free time (with talk). An hour of manual labor. The school had no janitors—we did it all. The floors were waxed and buffed and shined; everything was clean as a whistle.

And then, finally, an hour of recreation. This was required to be outside, a condition which of course drew no complaints from a bunch of energy-packed teenagers. Football, baseball, handball, tennis, hockey on the lake in the winter, or just time exploring the woods that surrounded the seminary.

After recreation and a shower came study hall from four to six. Chapel again. And dinner. We ate all meals in a refectory along with the priests and brothers, each of which had their own tables. We were assigned to a table that consisted of a senior, a junior, one or two sophomores, and two or three freshmen—six people to a table in all. Every important decision at the table was made by the senior—the lieutenant, you might say.

Only one person per table—a designated waiter who wore an apron—was allowed up at a time. The waiter picked up the food from a warming cart and brought it to the table.

Each platter had exactly six pieces of food. If it was dinner, we might have six (thin) slices of roast beef, six scoops of mashed potatoes, a vegetable of some kind. The senior took a portion (usually just one, though sometimes more than one), and passed the platter to the junior, then the sophomore(s), and finally the freshmen (which went according to alphabetical order). Some seniors, and occasionally a junior, decided to take more than their fair share. If the platter got to the last freshman and there was no meat or potatoes…tough luck. Those of us on the bottom of the food chain would usually split what was left.

We were assigned to a table quarterly during the year and, occasionally, we might end up with a senior or junior who would pass on the meat or potatoes (out of penance). The night's special bonanza was shared by the rest of us.

The same happened at breakfast and lunch. In the morning, we got a ration of six pancakes or six pieces of French toast—one for each of us at the table—with six strips of bacon or six sausage links. You might think that growing teenagers would starve on such a meager diet, but there were always three boxes of cereal, a pitcher of milk, a pitcher of juice, and a stack of bread on the table. No one walked away hungry.

Pat Johnson was in my class the year I started at Maryknoll. He was from Oklahoma, and a hell of a great guy. I ended up being assigned to a table with him a couple of times.

For all of us, there was something missing from our meals, something we had grown up with that we liked. In Pat's case, it was ham hocks and black-eyed peas. He petitioned Brother DeMontfort, who ran the kitchen and refectory, several times for ham hocks and black-eyed peas. Well, sure enough, after many months of gentle persuasion, out from the kitchen one afternoon for lunch came big bowls of ham hocks and black-eyed peas. Pat was in heaven. It was the first time I ever had that traditional southern concoction, but now we enjoy it regularly.

On another occasion, Pat had picked an armload of polk salad greens in the woods one afternoon. He brought them to Brother DeMontfort and asked if he would get the cooks to prepare it for him. Brother DeMontfort was hesitant, concerned that it was poisonous.

The school had three cooks who came in each day from St. Louis to prepare the meals. In general, they were rather rotund, but cheerful, black women. It turned out that polk salad greens are in fact poisonous, but not if you know how to cook them. Maybell knew how. The trick was to boil it, rinse it, and boil it a second time.

That evening a large bowl of cooked polk salad showed up on the table for Pat. When Brother Rene saw it, he pulled up a chair and as Pat put it, "The two of us ate a mess of polk salad that night!"

Dinnertime was always an experience. Father Allen, the Rector, sat at the priest's table with a bell like the ones in hotel lobbies. If he didn't like what he saw, he would slam the bell repeatedly, bing, *bing, bing, bing, bing, bing, bing*, then scream out whatever it was that was pissing him off.

He hated two things in particular. One was cutting bread with a knife instead of breaking it. (Bread was to be broken…period! Yes, even Wonder Bread). Off went the bell. The second was if he saw someone handling food with their fingers while eating. There was one and *only* one exception to the rule according to Father Allen: fried chicken, which was to be eaten with our hands, *never* by cutting it—that would draw another long string of bell slamming.

Father Allen smoked constantly. Back in the early sixties, smoking inside was common everywhere, including at the seminary. Father Allen rarely ate more than a few bites of his meal before he moved his plate aside and lit up a cigarette in an ashtray he kept next to his plate.

Cigarette smoking was part of life for most of us, too. Anyone sixteen or over was permitted to buy a pack of

Luckies or Marlboros or Camels in the small store that was open for twenty minutes after the evening meal. Moreover, twice a week, on Wednesday and Sunday, we had the rest of the afternoon off after manual labor. We were free to do whatever we wanted. There was a music room with comfortable chairs and sofas and a 1960s style console record player, *and* a half dozen large ashtrays for anyone who wanted to light up.

Classes could be tense, especially if you were not prepared. And all prep work had to be done in the study hall the night before. There were no parents to say, "Now, Johnnie, have you done your homework?" And no one to ask for help if the assignments seemed beyond our paygrade. We planned our studies and allocated our time by ourselves even at the age of fourteen when we started at the seminary as freshmen.

The freshman class was divided into two groups: the 'smart asses' and the 'dumb shits', or what Terry Nelson, one of my classmates, called the Vegetable Garden. Well…I was in the Vegetable Garden. Either way, the curriculum was mostly the same, though the pace was not quite as fast for those of us in the Vegetable Garden. We all took Latin, Math, Biology, and English Literature, although the smart asses also took Greek. Yet, even in my group everything moved fast. We learned the Latin language from top to bottom—declensions, conjugations, the works—then began reading Caesar in our freshman year, and *The Iliad* and *The Odyssey* by Homer in our second and third years, all in Latin.

I had two Latin teachers—Father Casey in my freshman year, and Father North in my sophomore and junior years. Both were enough to scare the crap out of a matador, though Father Casey was undeniably the worst of the two. He would walk solemnly between our desks and out of the blue would ask one of us to start translating. Then after a page or so, he would set his attack, "Translate," on someone else. Lord Almighty if you were not prepared.

Father North was also tough, but at least a sense of humor would show through now and then. Once, as he was walking among the desks, he proclaimed how lucky we were. "Look at you guys," he moaned. "Three squares a day, no heavy lifting. What could be better!" And then he would single someone out to translate. His favorite phrase when he was going over a point of Latin on the board was to say, "*Nota Bene!*" (pay attention) or "*Notate Bene!*" (pay close attention). And if someone had done a good job with the translation, he would merely say, "*Bene, Bene!*" When he wrote on the board, he would jot NB to emphasize a point—a notation I still use today.

In many ways, my time at Maryknoll changed my life forever. The monastic environment, the isolation from the world, no TV, few off-campus trips and visitors for four hours one Sunday a month, prayer, silence, meditation, all had a lasting effect on me.

Today, I need a certain amount of time hearing and feeling the silence and the thoughts in my head. And yet, soon after I left the seminary, I also left the Catholic church—and all forms of religion, in fact. None of it made much sense in a world where there was, and is, so much hatred, so many problems. If religion is such a glorious enterprise, why has it not brought peace to the world? I have many friends from my days in middle school at St. Francis Xavier who today call us to prayer when a member of our class is sick or has a medical problem. If praying can change the course of an illness, why does a benevolent God permit suffering and sickness in the first place? The suffering of children and animals...why? I have never been able to find a rational explanation for that.

At the end of my second year, I had doubts about continuing at the seminary. Tim Reilly, with whom I had originally come to Maryknoll, left at the end of his second year. I returned for year three but probably should have left sooner.

Little by little, a group of five or six of us started pushing the limit. Personal radios were forbidden (as was chewing gum). One of my friends, however, had smuggled in a small battery-powered transistor radio. At night in the dorm after lights out we would take turns listening with a small set of earphones. I remember tuning in Station KXOK out of St. Louis. The Beatles had just hit big, as did a handful of other groups. This was a new kind of music.

One day, a member of our small clique came up with a plan. We would get up late at night, go to the refectory, grab a bunch of treats, and head up the road to a small house called the Brother's house. It had been used by several of the Brothers who were overseeing construction of the seminary—now it was empty.

To avoid incrimination, I will keep the names of the participants unknown. In the dark of the night, I felt a nudge on my arm, "John, come on, we're going."

I slipped out of bed and crept out of the dormitory as if going to use the bathroom. We went to the kitchen and filled our arms with pickles, slices of cake, bread, salami, drinks, and headed up to the Brother's house. Sure enough, the door was unlocked. We went inside, sat on the floor of the empty living room, and talked and ate gleefully until very late. That was just one incident in a growing string of baleful events that kept us on the edges of the rules.

In January of my third year, when we all had returned from home for two weeks with our families, one of our group came back with a pellet rifle. He hid it in the basement behind a stack of suitcases and footlockers. Instead of playing baseball or football, we took to the woods every day for our hour of recreation, rifle stuffed under a jacket until we slipped into the nearby woods. We never did any real hunting—we just blew an old tin can off a tree branch or something else innocuous.

At the seminary, if you broke a rule, you had two options—one self-directed, one non-self-directed. In the first case, anyone who did something such as speaking during morning silence, for example, was obliged to own up to their gaffe and report themselves to Father Meehan, the Dean of Discipline, after the dinner meal. This would usually garner some form of minor penance.

Alternatively, if you were *caught* breaking a rule (speaking, for example), you might be told by a senior to report your infraction after the dinner meal. This would generally lead to a slightly more severe penance. Penances ranged from saying a rosary to the most dreaded one—penal squad—which meant that the offender had to work during the recreation hour.

In the case of the pellet gun, none of us reported ourselves, of course. Then one day after dinner, Father Meehan called the group of us up to see him. We dutifully stood before him as he said, "William…do you happen to own a pellet gun?"

"Yes, Father," William replied.

"Well, you don't anymore," Father Meehan firmly stated.

And with that came the verdict of penal squad for a week for all of us. We left the refectory, not a word spoken among us.

Now for the big confession and a very big *mea culpa*. And yes, my colleagues who also embarked on this adventure will once again remain unnamed. I am not even sure what prompted us to do it. It so happened that for manual labor I had been assigned as a sacristan. In all there were six sacristans, ranking from first sacristan (the top dog) to the sixth sacristan (the grunt at the bottom). My only task was to fill the cruets for the priest with water and wine for morning mass.

There were roughly fifteen priests at the seminary, some had been assigned to teach, a few were on a furlough from mission duty before they would return once more in a year's time. All of the priests said mass in the morning at small altars with an assigned altar boy. The wine for the cruets came from a gallon jug. When the jug ran low, I would get another one from Father Mueller, who was in charge of the sacristy.

So one night, we did not make our way up the road to the Brother's house. Instead, the group—probably five in all—crept into the sacristy. We were all sixteen. We sat on the floor. I pulled the jug of wine from the cabinet. It had a squirt attachment to make it easy to fill the cruets. We started drinking small squirts of wine. Not much seemed to happen, though I think we all expected to get buzzed right away. Okay…another little squirt now. Around went the jug. Time passed; I don't remember how long. And another shot, a little more this time. And another. Then it started to hit. Whoa, whoa! I was feeling wobbly, everyone was. We sat with the jug between us, taking liberal hits of wine and trying to be quiet.

The priest's rooms were on the floor directly above us. I'm not sure how we managed to remain quiet throughout our nighttime bender in the sacristy, but one thing was sure, had we been discovered, we would have been swept out of the seminary instantly.

I looked at the jug. Oh shit, no, we had taken it down by almost half. This was *not* good. I would need to procure a new jug from Father Mueller sooner than usual. He had told me that when I needed more wine to just go into his room and grab one from the closet. He didn't mean, of course, after we had celebrated late at night in the sacristy.

Several days later I was heading out of Father Mueller's room when—wouldn't you know it—he was coming down the hall in the other direction. Seeing the new jug of wine I was carrying, he stopped, looked quizzically at me, and said, "John, didn't you just get a jug not long ago?"

Now what? I shrugged as if I couldn't remember.

Father Mueller did the same and went on.

I knew at that point it was time to leave the seminary. I had already mentally gone but officially did not leave until the end of the year.

10

WORKING AT JEWEL AND THE PERFECT CRIME

When I turned seventeen, I wasted no time applying for a job at a very large supermarket called Jewel—or as most of us knew it, The Jewel. The Jewel food chain had been around in Chicago since the early 1900s. Originally known at The Jewel Tea Company, it consisted of small grocery stores throughout the city, one of which had been in downtown La Grange for decades.

A buddy of mine named Johnnie Martin worked at the store. Eventually, the company closed the small stores and opened large supermarkets, including one in La Grange. With Johnnie Martin's help, I managed to get a job working in the store, usually in the produce department.

I worked a couple of evenings a week after high school until ten o'clock, and on most Saturdays and Sundays for eight hours. We had a grand time working there. We all knew each other or made friends quickly with the other kids at the store.

I liked working in the produce department most of all and as time went on I managed to end up there on weekends. There were three of us who usually got the produce assignment. The three Johnnies as it were: me, Johnnie Martin, and Johnnie Campisi. (Lots of kids named John back then. Of course, it was a very Catholic neighborhood). We loved working with the produce managers, who for some reason seemed to be the most fun to work for at the store.

Johnnie Martin was one of those people who couldn't keep his mouth shut when a chance to wise off came along. One Saturday we were working diligently stacking and arranging apples, and oranges, and lettuce when a woman came up to Johnnie holding a peach.

"Excuse me, young man, is this a free-stone peach?" (Meaning the meat of the peach doesn't stick to the pit.)

Johnnie pulled a big Irish smile across his face and said, "That's right, ma'am, there's a free stone in every peach."

The woman was livid. She stormed out of the produce department and raged at the store manager, who as far as I know never said a word to Johnnie.

The store in La Grange was one of the busiest in the Chicagoland area. When I worked there, a burly Italian fellow named Ben Gazerra was the head store manager. Becoming a store manager at Jewel took years. It required working one's way up the ladder as grocery manager, produce manager, assistant store manager, then store manager at a smaller store, and then if the company was convinced, a store manager at one of the real gems like the new store in La Grange. It seemed like all the managers in all the departments were of Italian extraction back then, and there was talk that Jewel was owned by the mob, though I have no first-hand knowledge of that.

When I worked at The Jewel, we had an assistant manager named Joe Cusimino. A nice guy, serious but fun at the same time.

It was late in the summer and Ben was ready to take his annual two-week vacation. Joe Cusimino would naturally take over the reins while Ben was gone. Joe knew the ropes, and Ben had confidence in him. The first weekend that Ben was gone was just before Labor Day. The store was running specials on meat, vegetables, fruit, canned goods, just about everything in the store. Food was expensive back then. People would check the newspapers to see which stores had the best buys, cut out coupons for the discounts, and take them to the stores when they shopped.

I remember that particular Saturday very well. We were busy as hell stocking shelves and upfront bagging groceries in the check-out lanes.

The store was open until ten o'clock as always. At the end of the day, the store manager would take the receipts, checks, and cash and lock them in a safe for pick up by Brinks the next day. Remember, now, this was in the 1960s before the days of credit or debit cards—almost all transactions were done in cash, a few people paid with a check.

Joe executed the perfect crime. The standard routine at the end of the day was that after the store had closed and all the employees had left, the manager would take the money and lock it in a safe. Then, he would be the last one out the door. He would set the door and window alarms with a key after he left. Joe followed the routine to the letter. He locked the safe, left the store, turned on the alarms. Then he apparently got in his car and drove off to make it look like he was done for the night. Not exactly. Joe went back to the store, turned off the alarms, opened the safe, dumped the contents into a satchel, closed the safe, left, reset the alarms, and was gone. Gone with a whopping $200,000 dollars—close to $1.75 million today, adjusted for inflation.

In the morning when Joe didn't show up, the assistant manager opened the store and went inside where she found a totally empty safe. Nothing but a lot of air—lots and lots of it.

It appeared as though Joe had gone straight to O'Hare Airport with a plane ticket in hand and a bagful of money. Don't forget, this was before TSA, X-ray machines, and all the other check-in requirements of today. One needed only to show a ticket (and a passport if it was for an international destination), board the plane, and get your bag of honey-roasted peanuts and a cocktail.

Undoubtedly, Joe had managed to secure a fake identity and fake passport if he was heading out of the country. He needed merely to fly to some place like the Cayman Islands, deposit the money in an unidentifiable account, and spend the rest of his days being served mai tais under a cabaña on the beach.

As far as I know, Joe was never caught.

11

TAYLOR FORGE AND THE UNITED STEELWORKERS UNION

In the summers when I was eighteen and nineteen, my father got jobs for Roy and me at Taylor Forge, a massive steel forging company in Cicero, just west of Chicago.

Forge plants do not make raw steel from ore. They take steel sheets and heat them red-hot and then shape them either by pounding or repeatedly turning the hot steel on rollers to make pipes and flanges. The two primary finished products at Taylor Forge were round, flat discs such as those used for manhole covers, and metal pipes of all sizes and configuration.

Taylor Forge had four massive furnaces that were kept fired up around the clock every day of the year. To make a disc, a piece of steel was loaded into the furnace, heated to an extreme temperature, transferred to one of the 'German' hammers, which were huge pneumatically powered beasts. A large hammerhead would rise up fifty or sixty feet and with a thunderous blow smash the metal disc over and over until it had been thinned to the desired shape and tolerance. It was then taken out of the hammer to cool.

The pipes were made by placing a sheet of steel in the furnace, heating it red hot, and curling it on a set of rollers until it was a round pipe with barely a quarter inch gap between the two edges, which were then welded together. The size of the sheet determined the size of the pipe. The biggest pipes were about six feet long and four-to-five feet in diameter, either straight or curved.

So far, so good. Next step, the pipes were painted with a coat of non-rust grey paint.

Roy got one of the good jobs at Taylor Forge, working with a crew on a furnace. I got a totally sucky job painting pipes.

Taylor Forge was a family-owned company and was a long-time union shop. Everyone belonged to the United Steelworkers Union. It was obligatory, no option, and it was a good thing.

Mostly all the work at Taylor Forge was done as piece work. Operationally, this meant each job was rated according to how long the company and the union figured it would take to complete it. For example, if a job was determined to take one hour, then it would come with a ticket of 1.0. However long it took to do the job, Taylor Forge paid for one hour of work. If two hours of work were done in one hour, then Taylor Forge paid for two hours. For example, if Taylor Forge paid $2 an hour as its flat rate, then 100% of work for a forty-hour week paid $80. However, 200% worth of work during the same forty-hour week paid $160.

So, all the workers on the furnace always made 200% because they worked as teams of usually four people. Due to the extreme heat from the furnace, they were only permitted to work for twenty minutes at a time. Another team would replace them and the teams would rotate like that all day.

As for painting pipes, it was easy to make 200% painting the big ones, which might be rated at 1.0 hour and could be painted in twenty minutes or so. Piece of cake…if you were Stosh, that is!

When I worked at Taylor Forge, there was a fellow named Stanley—Stosh, to everyone at the forge shop. Stosh had come to the US from Poland. He lived in Argo-Summit, a working-class neighborhood on the southwest side of Chicago. You always knew if you were anywhere close to Argo-Summit because the Argo Cornstarch plant was there and the whole area and everything for several miles around smelled distinctly of corn starch. It also had lots of immigrants like Stosh from Eastern Europe.

Stosh was a nice guy, though we didn't talk much because his English was quite poor…and I spoke no Polish. The real problem for me, however, was that Stosh painted all the big pipes and left me with all the small crap that was hard to make much money from. I might have to paint twenty-five pieces just to get one hour of piece-work time.

Occasionally, there were stacks of even smaller pipes that required fifty or sixty to get credit for just one hour. It was next to impossible to make 200% for a day's work.

Then my big break came. Stosh took his two-week vacation and guess who was left to do the painting?

Well, on Monday morning at eight o'clock I started painting like a man possessed. I didn't stop for my fifteen-minute morning coffee break, or my fifteen-minute afternoon break, or the thirty-minute lunch break. I flew through one pipe after another non-stop for three straight days. I was *way* over 200% each day.

When Thursday arrived, I was still painting as fast as a son-of-a-bitch—slapping paint on one huge pipe after another as quickly as the forklift drivers dropped them down. Someone clearly realized what I was up to (probably one of the drivers). In the morning, a man came up to me while I was sloshing paint onto a pipe. He introduced himself as the union steward.

"How many tickets you got?" he asked, quite pointedly.

I pulled them from my back pocket and handed them to him, still painting to beat hell.

He tallied the hours. "How many tickets you got in your locker?" he said. We kept our tickets for the week's work and turned all of them in on Friday.

I stopped and looked at the man. "I don't know...a bunch," is all I said.

"Well, you're not gonna to turn them all in this week."

I returned to my work. "Why not? I painted the pipes."

"Doesn't matter, you're not turning them in."

I stopped and looked at the man. "So, what am I supposed to do with them?"

"Turn in eighty hours this week. Keep the rest and turn in eighty next week as well."

I shrugged. "What do you want me to do now?" I asked.

"Just paint the expedites." (The pipes that had to get out for shipment right away.) "Spread the rest out so you have eighty hours this week, and eighty hours next week. Capiche?"

I nodded. I was not about to take on the United Steelworkers Union.

"Look," he said, a little less aggressively. "This is one of the worst jobs here. No one wants to do it. Stosh has done it for sixteen years. He makes a living doing it. He feeds his family doing it. All the piece-work rates are reviewed and renegotiated each year between the union and Taylor Forge. If you turn in all those tickets, it will blow the hell out of the rates for Stosh. Would you want to do this crap for the rest of your damn life? Would you? No. No one does. That's why Stosh does it."

I nodded.

"Enjoy the rest of your week," he said, and left.

When I thought about it, I realized the union steward was, of course, right. It was the first time I realized how important unions are for workers. Taylor Forge was a model company in the way it treated its employees, but some of that had to do with the influence exerted by the union.

From then on I didn't feel so bad painting crappy little pipes while Stosh got all the big ones. At the end of the summer, I would be heading back to school. Stosh would still be slapping paint on steel pipes, taking his morning and afternoon fifteen-minute coffee breaks and his thirty-minute lunch, having a cigarette sitting by himself on a couple of pallets in a bleak corner of the forge shop.

12

CIRCLE CAMPUS, THE SDS, AND GETTING DRAFTED

After I left Maryknoll, I finished my senior year at Lyons Township High School in La Grange, and then enrolled in a two-year junior college (a community college today). I had no real idea what I wanted to study, or what I wanted to be, but I remember sitting in the guidance counselor's office as he paged through my Maryknoll transcript.

I could tell he was confused. What kind of defective high school offers no physics, no chemistry, some strange version of generic biology, a touch of math, and was packed solid with Latin, philosophy, and theology, and was pretty good when it came to English literature?

In fact, during my senior year of high school in La Grange after I returned from Maryknoll, my only option for language was still another year of Latin. I was in a class of twelve students, almost all of whom were female, a small contingent of sophisticated language students.

Additionally, in an effort to rectify my science deficiencies, I was put in a fusion course consisting of elemental physics and chemistry—Physics for Poets as it were. It was taught by the worst teacher of my life. A mean old geezer—burned out, scratching off the days until retirement, no doubt. Most classes, he spent the hour insulting us dimwits, realizing that he was stuck with the lug-nut crowd when he could have been teaching the whiz-kids about to float off to some nifty ivy league school in a few months. He was bitter and degrading; most of the students couldn't wait for the bell to ring. We wanted to climb under the desk while we were being insulted in his class.

My initial instinct told me to be a writer. I loved to read and, besides, it seemed like a nice, loose, amicable profession. I knew that Ernest Hemingway had grown up in a stylish three-story house (or as Hemingway might have said, "a swell house") in an upscale part of Oak Park, Illinois not far from La Grange.

One Sunday afternoon, I drove to where he had lived and stood there in quiet reverence for quite a while. I could almost feel the presence of the bigger-than-life Hemingway who had marked time in Parisian cafés and had fished in Key West, Bimini, and Cuba from *Pilar*, his elegant wooden cabin cruiser. I remembered the sense of youthful discovery that he detailed in his classic memoir, *A Moveable Feast*.

I enrolled in a round of classes: English Literature, Government (as it was called then), and Biology 101 and Chemistry 101, the latter two with an inner sense of dread after my lack of exposure to it at Maryknoll and my horrendous experience the year before in high school. But now everything flipped. English lit was fine. Government was utterly dreadful, not because of the content which I generally liked, but primarily because throughout the previous ten months I had grown my hair long, and long hair in 1965 had become a symbol of rebellion. Now again, for a second time, I encountered a teacher who poured out vitriol in the classroom, this time attacking and ridiculing anyone with long hair and using her position to promote hawkish conservative attitudes. I hated the class and despised her.

And yet for the first time in my life, I loved biology and chemistry, and a lot of that had to do with two great teachers. Mr. Stieger for biology, and Mr. Love for Chemistry.

For the first time, molecules, formulas, periodic charts, and science in general made sense and had real purpose. As simple as the lab assignments were in the junior college biology class, they were still far better and more educationally valuable than cutting open a formalin-marinated bullfrog or worm as we had done at Maryknoll while Father Allen paced anxiously among us, wanting to get out for his next nicotine scrub.

I finished two years of junior college in the spring of 1967. I had moved out of the house and was living in Brookfield in a small, dark, basement flat with a close friend of mine, John Kriva, whom I had known from my time at

St. Francis and at junior college. Brookfield was just east of La Grange—a simple, clean, working-class neighborhood.

In the fall, I enrolled at Circle Campus in Chicago, which was part of the University of Illinois system. It had acquired its name from the unique architectural design in which all the buildings were accessible from the ground floor as well as from above on a concrete second level that circled the campus. It made it possible to hustle from building to building out of the rain and the heavy winter snows.

It was truly an elegant design, yet in a city of towering skyscrapers, it always struck me as still one more piece of stone and mortar in a big concrete jungle. Nonetheless, Circle Campus had its advantages, it was cheap and accessible via the Burlington from Brookfield and La Grange to either Union Station downtown or the Halstead Street Station.

By the time I enrolled in the fall, I had convinced myself that a pre-med major was for me. In my first semester, I took a heavy load of sixteen hours, at least half of which were in solid science courses. Now I was flying—the kid who once barely knew where kidneys were inside a rubbery bullfrog was cruising through molecular biology.

1967 was during the peak of the Vietnam War. At age eighteen, every male had to register with the Selective Service Administration within two weeks of their birthday. Failure to do so guaranteed a knock on the door by the FBI with an invitation to jail time as a draft dodger.

But for anyone who did register, a draft card soon arrived in the mail, marked on it with your draft status. The four categories were: 1-A, eligible for service; 2-S, student deferment; 3-A, family hardship deferment; and 4-F, physically unfit for service. My card came back stamped 2-S. All I had to do was maintain a GPA of 3.0 or better and enroll in sixteen credit hours per semester.

This I did. Everything was going along well…for a while. I wasn't causing trouble and wasn't getting into trouble. I was there to learn.

In the mid-1960s, Circle Campus was a known hotbed of dissent against the Vietnam War. It had a sizeable membership of the Students for a Democratic Society (SDS). There were daily protests that always drew large crowds in the student union between the SDS and the Marine Corp Recruiters.

When I was not in class, I was watching the contentious debates in the union. I am quite sure the crowd was infiltrated by moles who kept a tally of everyone in the vicinity whether they were participants or observers.

After about a semester of this, the government had had enough; they were going to put an end to it quickly. They did this in the most effective way possible. In mid-January of 1968, I came back to Brookfield to find a letter from the Selective Service Administration with a new draft card listing my status as 1-A—eligible for military service.

I was pissed! I didn't believe in the war. But then, hardly anyone my age did either. I had no urge to fight for a catastrophe that seemed to be spinning out of control more every day.

> The Young Socialist Alliance, the youth group of the Socialist Workers Party; the University of Illinois Circle Campus Committee to End the War in Vietnam, a group in opposition to the Vietnam War; and the Chicago area Draft Resisters, a group in opposition to the draft, set up a protest desk at the Student Union Center on the University of Illinois Circle Campus, Chicago, Illinois, on January 18, 1968. This action was taken to protest the presence on campus of Marine Corps recruiters on January 16 and 17, 1968.

The above is an excerpt from an FBI file released May 8, 1994 by the Freedom of Information Act. The FBI file was made January 23, 1968.

The next morning, I promptly showed up at the Selective Service office and wanted to know why, and how, I had been reclassified to 1-A when I was a student in good standing.

A woman took my card and looked at it. "This?" she said, referring to the classification.

"Yes, that," I griped. "I am a student at Circle Campus, and I had a 2-S classification...until yesterday, that is."

"Oh, ha, ha," she said, in a jolly tone.

I failed to see the joke.

"Don't worry about it. Just get a letter from the school and we'll have this fixed up in a flash."

I left feeling as though everything was fine. She had made it sound as if this happens all the time, and that it can be easily rectified. Yet, in the back of my mind, something did not seem right.

In the morning I rode the train to Halstead Street as usual and walked the seven blocks to the university. I had barely arrived on campus when I saw a line of students. A long line going around one building and along a second one until it reached the office on campus that handled draft issues.

I had never been to the office; I had no reason to go, until now. I asked someone what was happening. He shook his head, waved a letter from the Selective Service Administration in one hand and a draft card in the other, which I assumed had been newly classified as 1-A.

There were hundreds of students in line, meaning that hundreds of students had been 'accidently' reclassified to 1-A. I moaned and took my place at the end of the line. Time crept bye, the line barely moved. One or two would be admitted to the building, fifteen minutes later, one or two came out. It went like that all morning. By about noon, people were getting impatient and frustrated. A few students shouted from the line, demanding to know what was going on. Then a few more shouted.

Finally, a woman came out of the office. She stood on the top step with a bullhorn.

Someone immediately yelled, "What are you doing?"

Speaking through the bullhorn, she said, "We're going

as fast as we can. There is nothing more we can do." She turned promptly to go back into the office.

In a loud voice, someone called, "What's going to happen to us?"

She stopped, came back, and through the bullhorn in a calm but almost stern voice, said, "You're going to get drafted." The words rattled heavily above us. She turned and went inside.

You could hear a pin drop.

At that time, there were many things about this I didn't know or realize. It was easy to figure out that the government wanted schools like Circle Campus, schools that fed the war resistance, to be neutralized quickly and at all costs. But what none of us knew then was that the war machinery in Washington was planning a massive military strike in Vietnam that would follow the cease fire of the Tet holiday. The government was losing more soldiers every day, and they figured the solution was to pack more GIs into the jungles and rice paddies.

My mind was a blur. I got on the train and rode it back to Brookfield.

It didn't take long for the woman's prognostication to come true. Within days, I received a letter from the draft board telling me to report Friday at seven o'clock in the morning at the Induction Center on Van Buren Street for a physical. I was to bring a paper bag with two sets of underwear and two pairs of socks. The implications were obvious. Pass the physical, ship out to boot camp that day. No visits back home to say goodbye.

On the day of the physical, I stood on the train platform at six o'clock waiting for the first train into the city. There were a number of others waiting also, all holding paper bags. Some with a wife and a child or two standing next to them. Being married was no longer a draft exemption—President Johnson, needing many more bodies—ended the marriage exemption in 1965.

The train arrived, we climbed on.

I went through a day-long examination, moving in line from one station to the next. When we got to the place where we were to have our hearing checked, we were each shut in soundproof booths where we put on a set of headphones and were told to press a button every time we heard a sound. Apparently, a bunch of inductees had concluded that this was their way out of the army. No, 'Good Morning Vietnam' for them!

They pumped the button randomly until the person running the test had had enough. Blasting through our headphones came the warning, "Okay, you assholes, you *cannot* flunk this test! It is *impossible* to! But it will guarantee that you spend thirteen months slogging your way through a jungle in Vietnam with a rifle."

As far as I could tell, everyone's hearing suddenly

became near perfect.

The rest of the physical left no special memory for me except that I recall that no one talked, smiled, made eye contact. We were sheep moving along one step at a time, stopping briefly, then another step.

The mind turns inward when it knows something lies ahead that we would like to avoid. Everyone knew the five-hour ordeal would end with a short bus ride to Union Station and a longer train ride to boot camp somewhere. Young men eighteen, nineteen, twenty years old thinking about the wives and children they had to tear themselves away from on a bitter January morning to rush to the train before it left. No one had thoughts or illusions of going off to be a hero. No one was Audie Murphy that morning.

I eventually arrived at the last station after every inch of my body had been poked, probed, and checked. The room was dimly lit. It had two sets of raw wooden benches against the back wall and a couple of scratched government-issue desks up front where three army doctors, who were not much older than we were, sat. As we went through the physical, we carried a set of papers that were stamped at each station. I paid little attention to it, most of it meant nothing to me.

One by one, people were called up to one of the doctors who paged indifferently through their papers, stamped it, and sent them back to the bench again.

My name was called. I went to the desk where a doctor gave me a very pissed-off look and snatched my papers from me. He quickly, almost haphazardly, reviewed them, stamped the front, handed them back to me, and said, "Go."

I stood silent for a second. "Go? Go where?" I uttered. I assumed he meant back to the bench with everyone else who had passed the physical and would be heading to boot camp.

"Go," he ordered again, this time louder.

Still not knowing what he meant, I said, "Go where?"

Finally, he looked at me and all but yelled, "Get-the-hell-out-of-here!"

I looked at my papers. On the top was stamped 4-F, unfit for military service.

What I later realized was that early in the physical we filled out a short form that included any possible impairments we might have. I checked off that I had been hospitalized in traction with severe lower back pain. When I got to one of the stations, a doctor told me to go get an X-ray. He read the X-ray, scribbled something on my chart, and aimed me back into line. As I went along, I read the obtuse words: Almost grade 3 spondylolisthesis, lumbar vertebrae 4-5.

Later, I looked this up and found that I had two misaligned vertebrae, one of which was cracked, that were putting pressure on the nerves coming off my spinal cord.

I walked out of the induction center and for the second time in several weeks took the train back to Brookfield with my mind in a blur.

I had not told my parents about my date at the induction center. Had I been drafted—which I was certain would happen—I would have given them a call from a phone in boot camp somewhere.

13

MEMORIAL HOSPITAL

John Kriva was happy and shocked to see me when I returned from my induction physical that day. He wanted to celebrate; he pulled two cold beers out of the refrigerator and popped them open. Although neither of us was yet twenty-one and thus unable to buy beer legally, John always managed to procure it from a refrigerator his father kept filled with beer in the garage.

I thought about the irony of the fact that most of the people who went through the line for a physical that afternoon couldn't buy a six pack of beer but were deemed old enough to participate in a war halfway around the world. A war that grabbed young men out of society and sent them to fight and maybe kill, even though they could not yet vote. The voting age was not changed from twenty-one to eighteen until the 26th Amendment was ratified in 1971 when the Vietnam War was already lost and the US was getting out anyway. What did the bastards running the government care now if most of the eighteen-year-olds decided to throw them out of office? They had already succeeded in recklessly propagating the war effort for well over a decade.

I took a slug of beer but didn't feel much like

celebrating. The empty faces of the young men at the drab green induction center waiting to be taken to boot camp filled my thoughts. I learned later from many friends of mine who had been drafted that they would never be quite the same after they returned as they were before. Some would hold their experiences quietly to themselves. Others would struggle with them the rest of their lives.

I never returned to Circle Campus. I had missed two months of classes and exams that I could not make up. Nor did I have the stomach to watch the high-tension jowlings between the SDS and the military recruiters. I was too pissed-off about the war to watch it debated day after day.

But I needed income, so I began hunting for employment. Anything would do, I had no enthusiasm in my search for work, I really didn't give a damn what I did.

I had heard that the local hospital had openings for various menial jobs, so I applied for a position as an orderly and was hired. It was not a job that took much training—helping the nurses on the wards, some bedpan duty, now and then work in the OR or the ER.

But simple as the jobs were, they suited my needs. My days were sometimes enlightening, sometimes disappointing—sadly so. For example, I remember arriving at seven in the morning many times and clean out one of the OR suites that had been used during the night for an emergency D&C. At the morning staff meetings, everyone sat stoically as the night anesthesiologist and nurse reviewed the case. I came to learn that D&Cs were usually done after miscarriages, but I was surprised at how few were done during the day, and how many were done at night or in the early hours of the morning. Something didn't add up. Emergency D&Cs? Really?

Pretty soon I realized that they were not being done to stop the bleeding after a miscarriage. They were abortions performed in a sterile operating room for those who could afford them in the days before Roe v. Wade.

Then too, I had another even more personal experience with pre-Roe v. Wade. One afternoon a friend of mine, Will, showed up at my apartment in Brookfield.

"John, I'm desperate," he said. "I need help."

"Sure, Will. What's going on?"

"Sally is pregnant. She's decided to have an abortion."

I told him what was happening almost nightly in the OR.

"That won't work," he quickly said. "You need to know someone for that. You need connections. You need a doctor who is willing to do it in the OR. We don't know anyone."

I waited.

"Sally went to a doctor who will do it in his office during the day. He told her she needs to schedule an office appointment, and that she needs to come in through the front door and check in at the front desk like everyone else. She is to sit in the waiting room as if she's just there for a routine exam or something until she's called. She must bring a thousand dollars in cash. A thousand dollars...*in cash.* Ten one hundred-dollar bills in an envelope. He will do the abortion in the office. And then she must get up and walk out the front door like everyone else."

A thousand dollars is a lot of money today. It was an astronomical amount in 1968.

"Sally made an appointment. We scraped up five hundred. We're still five hundred short. Is there any way—"

"Yes, yes, absolutely," I said quickly.

I went that day and cleaned out my bank account and gave the money to Will.

In 1973, abortions were made legal by the passage of Roe v. Wade by the Supreme Court. Forty-nine years later, On June 24, 2022, Roe v. Wade was overturned by the Supreme Court. Did this mean there would be no more abortions in the US now? Absolutely not. They would merely once again become class-restricted ordeals. Midnight D&Cs at community hospitals would always be available for those who had connections. Abortions would be done in doctor's offices across the country for anyone who could afford it. Not for a thousand dollars, but for five thousand, ten thousand, maybe twenty thousand dollars. The abortion time clock had instantly been reset.

I worked at the hospital for a year and had given up all thoughts of returning to Circle Campus or returning to college in general. At the end of the semester during the draft debacle, I received grades for the four courses I had been taking. I flunked all four and along with it went my desire to be a physician.

At the hospital, I liked working in the OR most of all even though it was messy and I did little but mop up blood from the floor and pull blood-soaked drapes off OR tables after a procedure.

Some of the doctors were fun, especially two Cuban anesthesiologist refugees. They sat at the head of the patient on the OR table and now and then checked oxygen levels and occasionally injected something into an IV, then unfolded a copy of *Sports Illustrated* or some similar magazine and started reading, looking up periodically to check blood gases or see how the patient was doing.

I was also frequently assigned to a medical ward that was run by a fun head-nurse named Ms. Reisse (pronounced Reezie). She was a short middle-aged bachelorette of Eastern European extraction, who commuted in every day from Cicero just east of Chicago.

Ms. Reisse liked to play jokes on me, and knowing nothing about medicine, I fell for most of them.

With the straightest face, she looked up from a chart at the nurse's station and said, "John, I want you to go down to Central Supply and get a rectal stopper."

"A rectal stopper?" I replied.

"Yes…a rectal stopper. They'll know what it is. It's kind of like a champagne cork."

What? Was she serious? "A rectal stopper?"

"That's right. A rectal stopper," she repeated. "Mr. McCarthy in 2502 has a real bad case of diarrhea."

I shook my head in disbelief.

"The folks in Central will know what it is," Ms. Reisse said, still paging through the chart.

So, I went and dutifully requested a rectal stopper for Ms. Reisse on Medical Three.

Of course, the women who ran the autoclaves and doled out needles and bandages and other things from Central Supply laughed and roared and clapped their hands together until tears streamed down their cheeks.

"Oh, my!" one of them said. "Now you go tell Miss Reisse we *aaall* outta rectal stoppers. Went through a *whole big bunch of 'em* yesterday and now we waitin' for another shipment. But they be here anytime now. You tell Miss Reisse that."

The joke was very clear.

When I returned to the nurse's station, the staff was clustered in a group waiting for me, barely able to contain themselves.

You would think I couldn't be tricked again, right? You

know, 'Fool me once…', all that stuff.

But several weeks later Ms. Reisse said, "John, can I get you to go down to Central and get a left-handed cane?"

For all I know, today there may be such things as left-handed canes…technology and all! But in 1968, a cane was a cane: a stick with a curved handle and a rubber piece on the end. I went to Central, as requested, but it was the last time I was snookered by Ms. Reisse.

14

Turn-On, Tune-In, Drop-Out in the Age-of-Aquarius

While I was working at the hospital, I met a character through John Kriva named Al Dubinski. Al was a colorful person—part hustler part con, but always great fun. He worked at Pier 1 on Ogden Avenue in Westmont near La Grange. From Al, I met Bill Putnum. Bill was the manager at the store, which might have been one of the first of its kind in the Chicagoland area. Bill was a slim, hyper, highly energetic person—a chain smoker who went through a dozen or more bottles of Pepsi a day. He was older than Al and me by seven years or so, who at that time were both twenty.

Bill rented a modest two-bedroom apartment in a sprawling new complex on the south edge of Westmont. After Pier 1 closed in the evening, we would gather at Bill's. People, all about my age, came and went, making everything a gregarious, pot-filled, acid- and mescaline-tripping Age-of-Aquarius event amid daily anti-war demonstrations that raged throughout the city. Bill, himself, had been drafted, but it was prior to when the Vietnam War had heated up; he spent his two years on an Army base in Germany.

Everyone at Bill's was a caricature of a sixties flower child: long hair, bell-bottom jeans, maybe a tie-dyed T-shirt, sandals. And of course, everyone was overflowing with God-given hormones.

Bill kept the lights low, sometimes a psychedelic strobe or a small black light or a lava lamp lit the room in a preternatural glow. Rock music, protest songs, just about anything that was rolling out almost daily from the US and Britain—came out of a small but efficient pair of speakers on a record player.

I hadn't done much in the way of drugs until that time. I had smoked a joint or two with Al and John Kriva but I hadn't tripped. I don't know where all the drugs came from when we were at Bill's, but there was never a short supply. Al and his friends always seemed to have an endless bounty. And since the mantra of the time—'Free-Love, Free-Beer, Free-Food'—was at its zenith, everything was 'Share and Share Alike'.

I remember one of the first times I tripped. It was on mescaline that a friend of Al's had. Three of us dropped a tab. Bob Dylan was croaking *Like a Rolling Stone* on Bill's record player. In thirty minutes, the world around me changed. People assumed a multitude of odd looks—heads like foxes or alligators or just their own head with the mouth of sockeye salmon but speaking in perfect round sentences. For reasons I didn't understand, all the women had a radiant sexuality I had not noticed before.

The three of us left the apartment heading for the *7-Eleven* to pick up eats and munchies. All three climbed into Jake's VW Bug. He drove down the street toward the store through a small subdivision that was nearly deserted at that time of night. America was watching the blue tube or already sound asleep.

Anyway, Jake had forgotten to turn on the headlights. But it didn't matter. It was as if we had the vision of a cat. The whole neighborhood, the streets, the houses, everything, was perfectly lit, almost glowing. Bright and colorful in shades of peach-orange and purple and jade green, blending and separating. Jake was driving slowly, probably too slowly, creeping down the road like a large caterpillar. If there were other cars, I don't remember seeing them. When we got to the store, Jake went inside and bought an armload of chips and candy and other crap and we returned the same way down the street again and made it safely back to Bill's.

Most of the drugs consisted of weed, hash, acid, or mescaline. There was very little coke and not many cokies came to party at Bill's, probably because coke was expensive relative to the other available highs.

Unquestionably the single most memorable moment of that time was one night at around nine o'clock. I walked into Bill's. Everything was as usual. People I recognized, people I didn't. The lights, the music. A small group was sitting on the floor passing a hash pipe between them. One barely needed a toke off the pipe to get high, the air in the room being as distilled with the fragrance of the hash as it was.

Grace Slick was rolling out the words to *White Rabbit*, a more perfect song there could not have been. A girl who herself was the spitting image of Grace—bangs to her eyes, brown hair to her shoulders, electrifying cosmic look—danced slowly in the middle of the room, singing to the song.

I was straight and sober when I entered Bill's and yet it appeared as if Grace Slick was right there before me, swaying and singing to the drumming beat of Jefferson Airplane.

I had seen this person quite a few times at Bill's, her name was Sybil. She often came alone or occasionally with a girlfriend or two. She knew Al, as did nearly everyone who came to Bill's. Al had a loyal and large contingent of followers. Sybil was young, maybe eighteen, could have been seventeen, uncommonly attractive and always intensely seductive—hair, face, eyes, everything. But tonight, more powerfully so than ever. She sang to *White Rabbit*, moving in the most alluring and captivating way in the shifting glow of the shadowy, almost eerie, room.

The second I walked into the room Sybil's eyes locked onto mine. She moved slowly over, stood in front of me, and continued singing, barely moving her head or body. Her gaze was engrossing. Her eyes, always crisp and clear even when she was stoned, were more vibrant and more penetrating and more riveting that night.

As the song came to its timeless ending, she sang "…remember…what the dormouse said…*feed* your head…*feed* your head." She took my hand and in the palm she placed a tab of mescaline. I swallowed it without giving it much thought. Together, we went to the side of the room and sat cross-legged facing each other. The music continued: Barry McGuire's *Eve of Destruction*, Bob Dylan's *A Hard Rain's A-Gonna Fall*, and *The Times They Are A-Changin'*. The mescaline began to circulate through me, I felt an extraordinary oneness with this person I hardly knew.

We spent the rest of the night in Bill's vacant second bedroom that had a thin double bed mattress on the floor. After that, I sporadically saw Sybil at Bill's in the evening. When she came in alone, we would get high and make a visit to the spare bedroom, though we never saw each other much except at Bill's.

I felt quite sure Sybil was bisexual. She had a friend who stopped by now and then with her whose name was Roxanne but went by the name Rocky. She was a petite Hispanic girl about Sybil's age. They worked together as waitresses at Barone's, an Italian restaurant in Countryside, south of La Grange, that was famous for its pizza.

One night at Bill's as I sat next to Sybil taking hits off

a hookah that was making the rounds, she blithely asked if I had ever had sex with two women. I confessed I hadn't. A glimmer of discovery came to her eyes. I already suspected from our previous conversations that Sybil had experimented extensively with sex; I figured she was setting the stage for a *ménage à trois* with me and her and Rocky.

Of the two most common psychedelics, LSD and mescaline, I preferred mescaline. Though both were (and still are) used recreationally, neither is addictive, although tolerance can develop with frequent use. In truth, I never really took either of them all that often.

In 1967, LSD and mescaline were legal. The highs, which were somewhat similar, had their own subtle differences. LSD, lysergic acid diethylamide, is a synthetic drug. Visual hallucinations and illusions, called trips, and a feeling of euphoria are common features of the drug, although the trip can turn dark, something I never experienced. Flashbacks can occur, particularly when the drug is taken frequently. LSD is considerably more potent than mescaline in its ability to induce an altered state of consciousness. Having used both, I preferred mescaline for its soft, ethereal, and pleasant visually enriched experiences and mind excursions. One notable difference between the two was that LSD, being synthesized, was more predictable in duration and effect than mescaline, which was rather loosely prepared from peyote and other hallucinogenic cacti.

Although it was a time riddled with drugs and sex, it also was an age when a whole generation was ardently searching for answers to every aspect of life. The reasons for this have been studied endlessly by scholars who know more about it than I do. The common explanations, the war in Vietnam and drugs, were certainly major contributing factors. However, I feel quite sure that much of it was also due to the unfettered upbringing of the baby boomers.

So, even with the bounty of drugs (and sex), we somehow retained enough sensibility to occasionally probe life—its meaning, purpose, and value. Bill became our grand master, a guru—someone who listened and disseminated shards of intellectual brilliance, always given out sparsely. He had a way of bringing every question forward to ascertain its significance. Some nights, hours would pass like minutes as we sat, talked, and listened.

I would remain at Bill's until late, one or two in the morning and then head back to my apartment, sleep a few hours, and be at the hospital again bright and early for my shift at seven o'clock. Doing this day after day was easy, a snap. Today, to do it even once makes me shuffle through the day, feeling like I've been dragged through a knot hole.

1968 turned out to be a dreadful year. In February, Edward Kowski, one of my sister's friends, was killed in Vietnam. Mike Reilly, the brother of Tim Reilly whom I went to Maryknoll with, had been killed in Vietnam the previous year. Martin Luther King was assassinated in April of '68, and Bobby Kennedy fell to a bullet shortly after in June of '68. With the war in Vietnam heating up more each day, the Summer of Love of 1967 had become little more than a memory from which nothing positive had come forth. The glorious intentions of our generation were turning sour minute by minute.

The Democratic Convention was slated for August 26-29 in Chicago. A large demonstration was planned for the final night. President Johnson had declined to run for re-election, but he was by no means out of the picture during the 1968 campaign. He pushed hard to get his vice-president, Hubert Humphrey, on the ticket.

We saw Humphrey as a clone of Johnson who would keep the war in Vietnam going, a coward unable to stand up to the Pentagon machinery that fed the conflict. Eugene McCarthy, who was unconditionally opposed to the war, was the clear choice of most of the younger voters.

Johnson had wanted the convention to be held in Houston, but Mayor Daley succeeded in bringing it to the International Amphitheater in Chicago a couple of blocks from the Union Stock Yards. The convention center was an old building that not only bore the fragrances coming out of the stock yards, but with its poor ventilation inside, a reporter declared, "it stinks like a hippie's armpit."

Danny, my sister's boyfriend along with several of his

friends, planned to go to the demonstration. About seven o'clock in the evening they stopped at my place as they were heading downtown and asked if I wanted to join them. I had to work early in the morning but figured we'd be back at a reasonable hour.

We climbed into Danny's car. When we got near downtown, I had a bad feeling that a lot of trouble was instore for the night ahead.

Demonstrators had collected throughout the city at Lincoln Park and Grant Park and near the convention center. When we got into the city, the streets were mobbed with people everywhere. In all, about ten thousand people showed up to protest the convention, consisting of a number of organized groups such as the SDS and the Yippies, the Youth International Party, as well as a large contingent of people like us.

Time went quickly, people were beginning to gather in groups. Someone in the crowd started speaking in a bullhorn. People were everywhere. I could sense that everyone was edgy and worried. Most of us came to protest, not to cause trouble. I was beginning to get worried. Danny and the others felt the same. Yet, nothing particularly bad happened until close to eleven o'clock when a melee broke out as thousands of the Chicago police came down the street in a phalanx carrying billy clubs. Everyone was pushing hard in every direction. I remember the night seeming to grow darker and more desperate as time went on. We all scattered. I got separated from Danny and the others and ended up jammed in with a bunch of people near the convention center.

The evening got more and more tense. More encounters with billy club wielding police who swung wildly for heads and hands and knees. As the sun was coming up, I managed to get on the EL and rode it west to the end of the line and picked up a bus from there, arriving home early in the morning.

The next day I learned that Danny also did not make it home until after daybreak. When Mayor Daley was asked by the media if the Chicago police were not themselves responsible for the rioting, he angrily answered in his classic way of misspeaking, saying, "Da Chicago police are not here ta create disorder. Dey are here ta *preserve* disorder."

If I had one regret from those days, it would be that the energy our generation captured about life, war, and the planet didn't stay with us as we moved forward through life decade by decade. But equally well, I often look around now and wonder what motivations drive young people today. There must be something, and it may just be that, not being connected to a group of people forty years my junior, I merely don't understand what it is. This much I know, however, there is another huge baby boom generation that is in the making as we exist today—the children of the current millennials. That new generation will someday be a force to be reckoned with on this planet, for better or for worse. We had our moment. We may have managed to stop the war in Vietnam, but then we turned inward, perhaps from exhaustion, perhaps from inertia.

Despite everything, Bill continued to be a source of sense and stability. He was an incredibly talented artist. One evening he said he wanted to do a portrait of me. For many nights he had me sit on a tall stool wearing jeans and a blue denim shirt and looking seriously significant while he made eight or so paintings in oil. I watched as they emerged day by day into the finished product. When it was done, I was shocked at the reality of the image, as though I might step right off the canvas and walk across the room, nod and thank him for the great job he had done, and gently walk out of the apartment.

Out of the blue, Bill said he was going to open a small 'head shop', just for the fuck of it. Maybe make a few bucks…who knows. Bill was always bursting with ideas; you never knew what would come next. So, he located a tiny store on Cass Avenue a block from the Burlington train station in Westmont, Illinois—and it was tiny, barely ten feet wide and all of thirty feet deep. It had a door and next to it a glass window at the front of the store.

Bill named the store *Up Tight*. He made an elaborate psychedelic painting and set it in the front window. It had the letters UP TIGHT tipping at all angles across the top with a caricature of someone who looked akin to Jerry Garcia's Doodah Man moving heartily across.

You entered through bead curtains into a room painted totally black, ceiling, walls, everything. Black lights gave the dayglow paint that decorated parts of the room an esoteric buzz. The store peddled all the usual paraphernalia of the day: hash pipes, jewelry, posters, tapes and records. Music by The Doors, *Break on Through to the Other Side* or something similar filled the tight air inside the store.

I frequently ended up working the cash register, though rarely was much money brought in given that the store was open only from six to ten in the evening. After several months, the City of Westmont got very uptight about *Up Tight* and made Bill shut it down for fear of contaminating the minds of the village teens, not realizing it was already too late for that.

My paternal grandfather, Robert Klein, as a young boy in Punxsutawney, PA, which at that time was a coalmining town.

Robert Klein worked most of his adult life driving a truck between Pittsburgh and Charleroi, PA. He had one of the first driver's licenses in Pennsylvania and was a life-long member of the Teamsters Union.

Wilma Zimmerman, my paternal grandmother. She married my grandfather in Pittsburgh. They had seven children. My father was the second oldest.

My maternal grandmother, who died before I was born. I have no pictures of my maternal grandfather.

My mother in 1941 in Mississippi. She and my father eloped when he was in Officers Training School in Louisiana.

My mother and father in Louisiana after they were married in 1941

My father as a 1st Lieutenant in Patton's Army in Europe. He is on the right with the five company officers. The company Captain is in front.

If I Could Do It All Again 119

My mother with me in Bensenville, Ill. in 1947.

My father with me (left) and Roy (right) in Bensenville.

Bensenville. Roy is on the left. I am on the right. My first experiment—growing corn in front of the house... Elation!

Maryknoll Seminary in Chesterfield, Missouri. I was in the first class in 1961 when the seminary had just opened.

Trying to look cool at Maryknoll. I'm third from the left.

Manual labor working with Brother Bart (on the tractor). I'm second from the right.

Mud wrestling at Maryknoll. Why waste a good puddle?

High-jump contest at Maryknoll.

Hope and me on the day we eloped in Chicago in 1971.

If I Could Do It All Again 121

Cindy, who went to Mexico with Skeets and me in Winnie.

Jane, my second wife, on one of our fun trips to the Caribbean.

Carl Galloway, MD, who married Hope after we got divorced. They moved to Los Angeles. While there, he became the subject of a *60 Minutes* segment about medical insurance fraud titled *It's No Accident*. He sued CBS and Dan Rather for $1.4 million but lost the case, not getting a cent.

Sebastian on top of the cargo boat going up the Amazon

Man with pet howler monkey, Iquitos, Peru.

Capuchin monkey, Iquitos, Peru.

Porters—Amazon rain forest.

Freddie Valles (right) explaining where we were going that day in the Amazon forest. On the left is one of the hammocks draped with mosquito netting and overlaid with palm branches in the event of rain. The porters threw this together the night before in a couple of minutes.

A porter at the front of the canoe going up a tributary of the Rio Napo. Sebastian is in the foreground.

Freddie leading the way into the jungle.

Medicine man from a local jungle village. Freddie stopped and called to him with a series of whistles. Soon, he came from the jungle and joined us for a while. As we were walking along, he stopped and uncovered a bunch of crocodile eggs.

Indian chief, Upper Amazon, Peru.

Freddie demonstrating the curare-tipped darts used with six-foot blowguns for hunting. One of the blowguns is resting across the top bar of the railing.

Passport entry, Nicaragua, 1986.

Pecking out the words to my first successful book on a Smith-Corona manual typewriter in Del Mar, California.

Me and Jeanne shortly after we were married in 2002. They say the third time is a charm. Now I believe it.

Jeanne today

15

HOPE OF THE CASTLE AND DRIVING A HACK

Basically, I liked working at the hospital. I continued to spend my nights at Bill's until I met a respiratory therapist named Josephine (Joey) di Cristofano. She was an Italian American beauty. Slim and svelte with a trim waist, narrow shoulders, well-proportioned ample breasts, light brown skin, hair that was full and thick and wavy dark, and black mysterious eyes. To top it off, she had ever-so-slight remnants of a few scars on her cheeks from teenage acne, which magically enhanced rather than detracted from her opulent sexuality.

Joey came from a large family that had moved to Clarendon Hills from a tight Italian neighborhood on the northwest ridge of downtown Chicago. Her father, whom I met once, had a stern, square face with eyes as dark as Joey's. He looked and talked like he had just walked off a Francis Ford Coppola movie set.

Joey and I had grand times *rolling like thunder under the covers* in my shabby Brookfield basement apartment almost every night. She was a year older than me, but she had the experience of someone ten years older. All-in-all, it lasted a mere six months, probably because...*we never did too much talking, anyway*, as Dylan had invoked.

Not long after, I started seeing a nurse named Margie, whom I had met when I worked in the OR. She commuted to the hospital from an Irish neighborhood east of Midway Airport. Margie, too, was older than me by about five years. Older seemed to be the order of the day at that time, though I never intentionally sought out older women. It's just how it happened.

Margie was married. Something I never really paid much attention to—nor apparently did she. Her husband was a naprapathic physician who practiced a form of homeopathic medicine. We would go out in the evenings when he was working. She would tell him she was going out with her girlfriends for drinks. Apparently, the story held water.

Having moved on from both Joey and Margie, I met an exotic knockout—Hope del Castillo, or more properly Esperanza del Castillo (literally, Hope of the Castle). Like Joey, she had caramel-colored skin, the same black hair (this time, straight and long), and the same sparkling black eyes.

Hope was working as a nurse's aide on one of the wards at Memorial Hospital. She came from a large family of eleven—nine children plus her two parents. They lived in La Grange, but were originally from the charming, provincial town of San Luis Potosi in Central Mexico.

Her parents had come many years before to Lafayette,

Indiana, where Hope was born and where her father earned a PhD in particle physics at Purdue University. He had done research and taught for many years at the University of Wisconsin at Madison and subsequently took a job at the Argonne National Laboratory that occupied a bucolic plot of land in Lemont, Illinois on the far west side of Chicago. Although they never flaunted it, the whole family dazzled me with their brilliance. All of the children, with the exception of Hope, eventually got a PhD or an MD degree.

I have always looked back at that time and laughed. Me, the grandson of coal miner immigrants in Pennsylvania. Hope, the daughter of a particle physicist. What an example of the prejudices and misconceptions people in the US have about who we are! I would always be the light-skinned, blue-eyed one with origins from Eastern Europe. No matter what, Hope would always be the person of color from Mexico. Nothing would ever change that in the eyes of many.

Not long after we started dating, Hope's family moved back to Mexico. Richard Nixon slashed funding for physics research, for reasons that were unclear to me considering that this was in the middle of the Cold War. In any event, Hope's father's job had been eliminated.

Hope and I started dating regularly. She quit her job at Memorial Hospital and worked briefly at the Hinsdale Tuberculosis Sanatorium. It was a three-story building with a large porch located on several hundred acres of land. Crazy to think today that in the 1960s such places still existed for the treatment of tuberculosis. After a couple of months, she took a job as a respiratory therapist at McNeal Hospital in Berwyn. I had lost interest in hospital work, bloody ORs and tricks from Ms. Reisse, notwithstanding. But fun as it was at the time, I learned that most medical work was terribly repetitive.

We moved into an apartment in Berwyn two blocks from McNeal. It was a second-story, three-room affair you entered from a set of wooden stairs that went up the back of the house, a place with all the ambiance of the sad apartment occupied by Ralph and Alice Kramden. We did our best to liven the place up: lime-green paint in the kitchen, bright orange in the living room. But it didn't really matter what color the walls were, we were happy.

I had heard that the West Side Cab Company was looking for drivers. I signed up and was hired for the night shift from six o'clock at night to six o'clock in the morning. There were only two shifts, each twelve hours, either day or night. It was hard to make money working less than twelve hours and, anyway, it was not a physically demanding job.

I made 40% of what was on the meter plus all tips. On an average day I would chalk up $50 on the meter ($20 for me) and another $30 or so in tips. It doesn't sound like much today, but $50 a night was good money back then. I usually worked six or even seven days a week and could bank 300 plus dollars.

I genuinely loved driving the cab, especially at night. There was something surreal and mysterious about going through the city—all over the city, north, south, west, trips to the airports—late at night. I loved driving slowly down the dark streets or through the mostly empty Loop in the early pre-dawn hours, everything surprisingly still and calm as the world moved past me.

Looking back on it, it was as though I was Robert De Niro with the voice-over dialogues as he went through New York City in Martin Scorsese's movie *Taxi Driver*. I have often felt that my time driving a hack through the sullen streets of Chicago was one of the best jobs I ever had.

During that time, three fares were especially memorable. I picked up a man in front of a building in the Loop. He was well-dressed and had a small leather suitcase and an expensive-looking thin leather valise.

"O'Hare," he said as he climbed in the back seat. He never said another word all the way to the airport.

Trips to O'Hare were always lucrative—seven or eight dollars. And you could count on a similar return fare. A couple trips to the airport guaranteed a better than usual night in the hack.

When we got to O'Hare, the man paid the fare. As he was getting out of the cab, he handed me a tip. I was shocked. It was a hundred-dollar bill. I was certain he must have made a mistake, probably figuring it was a single or possibly a five. I looked at him and held the bill up and explained what he had done. He turned to me, looked closely at the bill, said, "Keep it," and got out.

Several month later, I dropped a man off at a building in downtown Chicago. He paid the fare, handed me a tip, and vanished into the building. I was getting ready to stash the bill in the envelope with my other tips when I noticed that he, too, had given me a hundred-dollar bill. This time, however, I had no way of knowing whether he wanted me to have it or whether it had been a mistake. There was little chance of locating him in the sixty-story building.

I picked up the radio mic. "Eighty-four," I said, calling to the dispatcher using my cab number.

"Go ahead eighty-four," the dispatcher said.

"I dropped a guy off down here in the Loop. He handed me a hundred for a tip, then got out quickly. I don't know if he meant to give me that much."

"Hold it for three days," the dispatcher said nonchalantly. "If he doesn't get back to us, it's yours."

It ended up being mine.

I had no more hundred-dollar tips, but I had another unusual fare that was almost as good. It was around nine o'clock in the evening, as I recall. I was making the rounds through the Loop, up to the blues clubs on the near-west side, to a restaurant here and there in midtown. Small fares but good tips. Somewhere in downtown, three businessmen climbed into the cab.

"Racine, Wisconsin," one of them said, as they slid across the back seat.

It was clear they had been partying, and doing a pretty good job of it, yet they seemed more-or-less in control.

Racine was just across the Illinois-Wisconsin line about seventy miles from downtown. I knew other drivers had made these rare long hauls, but I never had one. I radioed the dispatcher and told her what I had.

She said, "Do it as a fare and a half, eighty-four. You will have to dead-head back (since it would be nearly impossible to pick up a fare in Racine). Don't run it on the meter. It would normally cost around sixty dollars, ninety dollars in all—total for all three. Get the money up front. That's it."

Sitting in the back, they could hear what the dispatcher had said on the radio.

I turned to them.

"Done," one of them said, pulling the ninety dollars from his wallet.

I headed out I-94, which went north into Wisconsin. The three in the back rode along happily, laughing and sharing a bottle of whiskey they had brought with them.

I found everything about driving the cab to be an adventure and I only got burned on a fare once, all from my own stupidity. I had picked up several teenagers near the Loop. They wanted to go to the southside, not too far away. A modest fare, all things considered. As I pulled over to where they wanted me to drop them off, before I could say a word, the doors flew open and they headed off in all directions.

After that, I was sure to get money up front from groups of teenagers if there seemed to be any doubt about what they had planned. Sometimes, they would give me a pissed-off look, hand over money for the fare, and climb in. Other times, they would hurl invectives at me and head off to find an unsuspecting driver.

On another occasion, I was going back into Chicago late at night on I-55, the Stevenson Expressway. There was a light drizzle of rain but there were few cars on the expressway. I was going at about the speed limit, roughly sixty miles an hour, when I saw a set of flashing lights in my rearview mirror—a Chicago police car. I pulled off to the shoulder of the expressway and waited for the officer to approach the car. He came over to the passenger's side, opened the door, and got in.

"Know how fast yer goin'?" he asked.

"About sixty, I think."

"Sixty-five," he said.

I didn't reply.

"Well, dat ain't so smart ta do in all dis rain. Coulda run

off da road, something like dat."

"Okay," I replied. No point in challenging one of 'Chicago's Finest', because dat ain't so smart ta do, iedda. I waited to see what he had in store. The last thing I needed was a ticket, a moving violation. At that time in Chicago, three moving violations resulted in suspension of your license for six months—a truly dreadful thing for a hack.

"Ya know," he said. "Da right ting for me ta do is write'cha a ticket. I mean dats what I should do…ya know?"

I sat and waited a second longer hoping he would give me the standard: "Okay, I'm gonna let'cha go dis time, but don't do it again." Or maybe he would just write a warning ticket, which would have amounted to nothing from a practical point of view. But I could see he was not about to budge.

"Well, I'm not sure what I can do," I said.

He shrugged, making it totally clear he was going nowhere.

I took out the envelope from my shirt that had my tips and removed a twenty-dollar bill and set it on the seat between us.

He reached over and quietly folded it and slipped it into his breast pocket. "Watch how fast yer goin'," he said. He got up and went back to his car.

16

A Candy Factory

While I was driving a hack and Hope was working at McNeal Hospital, we decided impulsively one day to get married. No elaborate wedding would there be. We would go to the courthouse and have a civil ceremony.

Papers were filed; bloodwork was done. Hope and I, and John Kriva and Sue, his girlfriend, who served as witnesses, went downtown to City Hall and waited our turn to see the Justice of the Peace. When we went into his office, he was sitting in his chair with his feet on the desk wearing a pair of white socks. He got up, asked a few questions, and went quickly through the ceremony which, if I remember, took all of ten minutes.

With that we were married. I told my parents about the marriage and Hope called her parents in San Luis Potosi. In fact, a couple of months later, Hope and I made a trip to San Luis. It was my first ever experience in Mexico, but I loved it and it would become one of many more yet to come.

San Luis is a charming provincial town in Central Mexico with beautiful old cathedrals and an elegant plaza.

Hope's family had a cook who prepared the afternoon and dinner meals, and it was there that I fell in love with a traditional Mexican Sunday meal of *Pollo con Mole*, chicken bathed in a rich, dark-black, complex sauce made with dozens of spices. Tortillas were bought twice a day from the tortilleria on the corner—fresh and delicious. Unlike any I had in the States.

I even accompanied one of Hope's brothers on a serenade he made with a few of his friends to his girlfriend's house late at night. They had guitars and lutes and sang Mexican love songs on the cobblestone street in perfect harmony. She came, joyously, to the second-story balcony above the street. It was straight out of a story book.

Feeling the need to get back to college, I enrolled at Elmhurst College a short distance from where we lived. I continued to drive the cab at night and took a class or two during the day, again majoring in biology. I went year-round and graduated in 1971 with a BA in biology.

Now, the time had arrived to get a more traditional job…the usual nine-to-five thing. But I learned quickly that few jobs were to be had with a meager bachelor's degree in science. I even went so far as to apply to the Central Intelligence Agency after I saw a notice that they were looking for candidates in all areas of science. I filled out the application and sent it in. Weeks later, I received a polite reply saying they were only hiring PhDs in biology (and psychology as well). I have no idea what a PhD in biology, or psychology, does in the CIA. The mind can only imagine.

So finally, I lowered my standards and began scrounging for jobs in quality control, mostly in the food industry. Besides the stockyards and meat-processing plants, Chicago is known for countless large candy factories that had set up shop there—everything from Wrigley's, to Mars, to M&M, to Nestlé, to Ferrara, and dozens more. And then there was the one I applied to: the Curtis Candy Company. Curtis had been churning out two candy bars, Baby Ruth and Butterfinger, since 1916 in a gigantic factory that stretched along the edge of I-294. *Everyone* in Chicago knew of the Curtis Candy Company.

I walked in, not really wanting to test candy bars for *Salmonella*, or for whatever unwanted guests found their way into the candy batches, but barely before I finished the application, I was offered a job.

I worked in Quality Control with two other people. Dave was the director; he rarely did anything but sit at his desk and read magazines about popular science. Clarence, a young black guy, had the specific assignment of testing for *Salmonella* and *Shigella*. He drove in each day from a southside neighborhood and was a great guy and loads of fun—a Vietnam vet who had been in Military Intelligence during the war. He had an infectious happy attitude and he loved to talk about the Cubbies and the Bears.

Me, my job was to do bacterial counts. I would throw crushed-up bars of Baby Ruth and Butterfinger into large bottles of milk broth, stick it in an incubator for a day, and streak what had grown onto agar plates. The next day I would count the number of bacteria that grew.

The candy manufacturing line in the factory went on for a half mile. The last step in the process after the bars had been coated with chocolate and chilled by passing through a refrigerated tunnel to harden the chocolate was for people on each side of the line to slip the bars into plastic wrappers. Obviously, this step was well before automation. But even so, Curtis turned out over a million bars a day!

One of the inspectors in the QC department in the room next to ours would take candy bar samples from the line and see how many finger and thumb prints they had.

On the other side of the 'bacti' lab was the R&D department; no place at Curtis was crazier. It had two employees whose jobs were to create new products. It was the test kitchen, so to speak. The director of the department was an immigrant from Slovakia named Mike Vaspalek; his right-hand man was Rudy Velone. Rudy was from the Philippines and was in the process of getting an MBA at Northwestern. Since he was nearly at the end of his degree, he worked full-time with Mike. The test kitchen had vats where they could mix huge batches of candy or dough or make anything at all. They had every imaginable spice, every imaginable ingredient. But there is no way to fully describe the weirdly exotic and barely edible crud they came up with.

Even from a hundred feet away in the room next to us, we could hear boisterous arguments spoken simultaneously in two languages—Slovak, and one of the hundred and fifty Philippine dialects, I don't know which, but it was clear that Mike Vaspalek understood not a word of it. Then, they would come marching through the lab with a tray of food, holding it delicately like a waiter in a Michelin five-star restaurant looking for people to sample their newest concoction. As soon as we got wind that a Slovak-Philippine fusion treat was making the rounds, the QC lab was suddenly empty.

Mike would stand with tray in hand and say, "Ver ees evy-von? Zey needs to try zees delicious tings Rudy and I have come up vit."

After about a year and a half at Curtis, the company decided to send one of us to Baltimore to learn a technique called Microanalytical Food Analysis. It was a method for detecting rodent hairs and insect fragments in food products. There had been a TV exposé that reported on *Bugs in the Batter*. Curtis wanted to get ahead of the game. So, Dave asked if I would take the course in Baltimore.

I told Hope what he had requested and a week later I was off to Baltimore for the course. It was conducted in a small laboratory called O'Dean Kurtz Associates. O'Dean Kurtz (O'Dean being his real first name), had spent a lifetime perfecting—in fact, pioneering the art of detecting insect contamination in food. He was *the* world expert. From a tiny fragment of a piece of an insect, barely a half millimeter in size, he could identify under the microscope the exact critter it came from. O'Dean was a small man in stature, barely five-six, but was an absolute whirlwind of energy.

When I returned to the candy factory, I tried out my new-found skills. It wasn't very exciting stuff, but it beat the routine of identifying bacteria in candy bars day after day,

One evening, a few days later, I got a phone call from Jim Gentry, an entomologist working for O'Dean Kurtz. He asked if I had an interest in joining their lab in Baltimore, claiming that I had done a good job of grasping the techniques needed. He offered a whopping salary of $9,600 a year—not so bad in those days and better than what I was making at the candy kingdom.

And so, Hope and I sat in our Ralph and Alice Kramden kitchen in Berwyn and talked over Jim's offer. It didn't take long before we both concluded, "Why the hell not?" It was a good chance to break away from the life we seemed to be stuck in. The thought of living on the east coast was tempting for a couple of Midwest landlubbers.

17

BALTIMORE

The Chesapeake Bay, steamed blue crabs, the Eastern Shore of Maryland, and oh yes, oysters and clams.

Everything went smoothly, mostly. We rented a U-Haul truck, loaded our VW Bug up inside, packed what little else we had around it, and took off for Baltimore.

My new job was all right, not the most exciting of my life, but not the worst either. Jim Gentry and I got along well. He had grown up in the Carolinas and had dropped out of high school and joined the Army. Twenty years later, he retired as a medical entomologist, having earned a bachelor's and master's degree while in the Army. Most of his time, he and his family were stationed in Kuala Lumpur, Malaysia, where he studied the mosquito that causes malaria.

If I learned anything about entomologists, it was that you are born one, you don't become one. The story was the same for every entomologist I met while working at Kurtz Associates. They had been picking up bugs from the time they were infants. Destiny had determined they would be an entomologist, and nothing would change that. Me, that's what set me apart as soon as I arrived at the lab. I knew I was not an entomologist, nor did I want to be one. Jim carried a miniature collapsible magnifying glass in his pocket. When we were outside, he would pick up a small bug, pull out the glass, and give you the exact scientific name of the little critter.

We moved into an apartment in Catonsville not far from where I worked. Hope quickly landed a job at the University of Maryland Hospital as a respiratory therapist. We made enough money to pay the essentials and have some left over for fun.

Baltimore was a different place in 1972 than today—safety in most parts of the city was not an issue, and so we began exploring the neighborhoods every chance we had. One of our first minor adventures happened not far from where we lived. We had learned that nowhere in the US are more blue crabs consumed than in Baltimore (which I found out from the locals was pronounced Balmer).

Blue crabs from the Chesapeake Bay were consumed almost by the bushels. The city was full of crab restaurants and local bars that, during the crab months, set a sign out front advertising steamed crabs.

When you went to one of the crab restaurants, called crab houses, you were seated at a plain table that had a sheet of white or brown paper on it, or sometimes just newspaper. You bought crabs by the dozen according to size. Back then, they were $8, $10, $12 a dozen, and the really big ones, the jumbos, $16 a dozen.

So, you decided which size and how many dozen you wanted depending on how many people were eating. They were always ordered with pitchers of beer. The crabs, steamed in Old Bay, were dumped on the table in a big pile. Get set for a two-or-three-hour ride into the world of fine eating. Picking every speck of meat out of a crab was (and is) an art—a true skill.

There were also small carry-out stores where you could buy live crabs to take home and steam yourself or get steamed crabs to take home to eat. Well, knowing nothing about the art of crab eating, Hope and I walked into a nearby crab shop and ordered "one crab". We got an empty, weird stare as if we had screwed up the order...which in fact we sort of had. Like in the restaurants, crabs in these stores were bought by the dozen. But, with little fuss, she wrapped one blue crab in paper. We took it home and together attempted to get the delicious Old Bay-soaked white meat from the crab. Hardly a meal, but now we knew what to expect.

Soon after, while wandering around downtown, we went to the Lexington Market—a wonderful public market with scores of vegetable and meat vendors and fish mongers. The market boasts of continuous operation since 1782.

In the center of the market was a square oyster bar where patrons bellied-up to a platter of freshly shucked oysters on the half-shell. Hope and I watched locals of all sorts as they devoured the oysters in ecstasy.

Being from the heartland, we had never had a raw oyster. In 1972, fresh seafood from the east coast rarely made it very far inland—unlike today when you can find anything and everything in supermarkets across the country.

I said to Hope, "What do you think? Do you want an oyster?"

She shrugged. Staring at the three oyster shuckers behind the bar as they set oysters on a half-shell onto plates of crushed ice, she said, "I don't know. You go first and tell me what it's like."

I gave a huff and pulled up to the bar. A black man wearing a rubber apron was shucking oysters and setting them on trays. He looked over and said, "Speak to me, my man. Speak to me."

"Uh…uh-huh…okay. Uh, I'll have an oyster."

He stopped shucking and looked at me as if he hadn't heard correctly. He said, "An *oysta*." He pointed to the pile of fresh unshucked oysters with his knife. "You want *one* oysta? Is that it?"

"Uh-huh, I think so."

He stared at me for a second, tilted his head, and said, "Well, ooh…kay."

He shucked an oyster, put it on a small plate and set it on the bar, then watched as I picked it up by the shell and slurped down the oyster as I had seen the others do.

"Whatcha think, my man?" he asked, as if he couldn't resist getting an opinion.

"Wow...that's pretty damn good," I said.

I looked at Hope. "Come on, let's get a half dozen. Three each. What do you say?"

So, we did. Two kids from Chicago, the *Hog-Butcher of the World*, had instantly become raw oyster lovers.

Six months after arriving in Baltimore, we decided to move from Catonsville into a second-story colonial brick apartment at 706 St. Paul Street in what then was an elegant part of the city. Of course, we had very little in the way of furniture, so moving was easy. It felt good to be in the city. It was close to Maryland General Hospital and an easy drive for me to Catonsville and back every day.

Around the corner was the Peabody Music Conservancy. The girl who lived above us was studying classical piano at the Conservancy. When she wasn't in class, she was in her apartment playing the piano all day and into the evening until ten o'clock when she was required to stop according to the landlord's rules.

On all the streets around us at that time were quaint old pubs and bars with good music and lots of people our age. A place we went to often was called The Classroom. It had a well-worn wooden bar and a big selection of beers on tap.

We also would frequently head over to Fells Point, a wharf at the top of Chesapeake Bay that had been servicing ocean vessels for centuries. Thames Street—a cobblestone street with saloons, bars, and pubs—ran the length of Fells Point. One of our favorite places was at the end of Thames called *The Horse You Came In On Saloon*, known to all in Baltimore as The Horse. The Horse dated back to 1775. Originally named Al and Ann's, it was Baltimore's oldest saloon and America's oldest continuously operating one—before, during, and after prohibition.

Additionally, The Horse was reported to have been the last stop of Edgar Allan Poe before he was found unconscious on the street in front of what was then Charity Hospital across from where Johns Hopkins Hospital is today. Poe was known to visit the saloon and get lashed on absinthe, a powerful liquor known for its almost hallucinogenic qualities. Poe's routine was to chug shots of absinthe one after another as quickly as possible until he was barely conscious, then stumble out and get a carriage to his house.

We spaced around Baltimore and down to D.C. and in the summer went to the Eastern Shore and became like the locals in no time. I quickly grew to like this east coast thing. It felt less confining than being squeezed into the middle of the country on the edge of Lake Michigan. We made friends, mostly people Hope worked with, and we partied together frequently, at least every couple of weeks.

After about a year, I knew I did not want to be picking 'gnat shit out of pepper' the rest of my life, and anyway, I wasn't an entomologist and thus never quite fit in with the crew at Kurtz Associates. But I also didn't want any more candy factory jobs. I couldn't drive a hack because I didn't know the lay of the land in Baltimore all that well.

In the meantime, everything was beginning to sour between Hope and me. Little did I know it, she was having an affair with a medical intern from the hospital—a person named Carl Galloway. (More about Carl later). I got to know Carl from our many parties together, but I suspected little until the bombshell was dropped by Hope. We eventually got separated and she got an apartment of her own, *conveniently* in the same building where Carl lived.

It was a heavy blow. I figured she would tire of Carl and head back to St. Paul Street, where I continued to live. But that never happened. As time went on, it became potently clear that the relationship was over. It was time to make a move, and a good time to dump the job at the insect lab, which I was beginning to hate more each day.

I did little at that time but drop into one of the neighborhood pubs as time drifted by month after month. It was in The Classroom that I met an energetically fun young African American girl named Mona. She was in her early twenties, a few years younger than me, and went to college in Baltimore. We dated for a while. One day—for no special reason—she suggested I come and meet her parents at their place on the west side of Baltimore. Yikes, I thought, is she serious? This could be tense as hell. When we got there, Mona walked into the house in her usual flamboyant way. Lo, they greeted me as if I were no different from anyone else Mona had dated. My heart suddenly started to tick at a normal pace again. We stayed for several hours. They were fun, happy people, exactly as Mona was.

I felt an urge to get out of the small apartment on St. Paul Street that Hope and I had occupied. I needed something different, something unique, some place I could go to and leave the world behind. I moved into a twenty-story high rise at 1111 Calvert Street, around the corner from St. Paul Street. I rented a place on the fourteenth floor (actually the thirteenth floor, which was skipped).

Life there was self-contained—exactly what I wanted. On the ground floor was a superb steak house with a terrific dark and moody bar—just the place to go at the end of the week and get plastered because the only thing you had to do was remember which button to push in the elevator to get home. A pool was on top of the building above the twentieth floor. This time, another elevator ride to the top deposited you at a place where a Saturday or Sunday afternoon could be wasted in a lounge chair only to get up periodically and refill a drink from the pool bar.

18

BALTIMORE CITY HOSPITAL AND DOWN TIME

Life was far from perfect but at least I had time (maybe too much) to reflect on what had happened during the past couple years of my life. Soon it became clear...I needed to move forward. Nothing in my past could be corrected now. I decided to go to graduate school in some area of biomedical research. Though the thought of becoming a physician left a bad taste in my mouth from everything I had experienced at Memorial Hospital, the idea of research seemed ideal. The question was, where would I go?

The University of Maryland offered a number of programs, as did other colleges and universities in Baltimore, most of which were state schools of one type or another. But as was usually the case, I wanted to go big. By east-coast elite school standards, Johns Hopkins University was a new addition to the group, having been founded in 1876 by Johns Hopkins, a bachelor Quaker merchant who left his entire estate of seven million dollars to the establishment of the school. (Johns Hopkins received his first name from his great grandmother's last name of Johns).

The University had two campuses. The main undergraduate and graduate schools were at Homewood campus a mile north of downtown. This was a possible option, but it meant a degree in basic science—biochemistry, physiology, something of that sort.

The medical campus was in East Baltimore. The Medical School had been built in 1889 after Johns Hopkins had died. Even before it was finished, however, it ran into financial difficulty. A group of wealthy Baltimore women picked up the bill, but only so long as the school permitted equal entry to women. It was one of the first medical schools in the US to do so.

The Medical School/Hospital has produced 18 Nobel laureates in medicine or chemistry and the university numbers 38 laureates overall.

I looked into various programs and decided the one that suited me best was at the School of Public Health. At that time, the school was named The Johns Hopkins University School of Hygiene and Public Health. A name that sounds weirdly strange today due to the reference to hygiene, though the school's origins in 1916 had led the way to improving the quality of health at a time when there was a desperate need in all areas of basic hygiene in the US. Since then, the school has consistently ranked as the number one school of public health in the country.

For years, despite considerable resistance due to tradition, there have been attempts to have the word Hygiene removed from the name, which was finally done in 2001 when the school became the Johns Hopkins Bloomberg School of Public Health, named after the financier Michael Bloomberg, who was an undergraduate alumnus of Hopkins and had donated several million dollars to the School of Public Health.

I got a school catalog and looked into the programs. Several sounded perfect for my interests; however, infectious disease epidemiology was enormously appealing. I went to the school and picked up an application and scheduled to take the graduate record examination, which the school required for admission.

Even if I got in, I would not be able to start for a semester, but I had no desire to put in a single day more at the insect lab. I had heard that Baltimore City Hospital in east Baltimore was looking for a lab technician to do basic hematology work in the ER on the midnight-to-eight shift. Baltimore City Hospital was a huge place, every bit the likes of Cook County Hospital in Chicago. I applied for the job and was hired on the spot.

More hospital junk, but at least only for a while.

The hospital lab staff gave me a CliffsNotes version of hematology: differential counts, blood smears and hematocrit tests, making cultures of all sorts. The hospital had a large lab that was used during the day, but at night the work was done in the ER itself.

The hospital ER was a blitzkrieg of non-stop motion all day and all night. It was separated into two halves, the surgical side and the medical side. Each was staffed with a few nurses. All the residents came from Johns Hopkins Hospital. They did rotations that lasted thirty days consisting of one day (24 hours) on and one day (24 hours) off. Back and forth like that for an entire month.

My lab was a tiny ten-by-ten-foot room between the medical and surgical areas. It had a bench, a small centrifuge for preparing specimens, equipment for making hematology slides, a microscope, and a dart board that was used mostly by the residents late at night.

One of the nurses was a fellow named Joe Morgan, who went by the name Mo. He was a male nurse who had earned his stripes in Vietnam as an Army corpsman. Mo had resisted getting drafted by applying as a conscientious objector, which most of us knew all too well back then was a futile endeavor. In any event, after being drafted he requested assignment as a corpsman, figuring he would end up in some semi-civil MASH unit away from the fighting. Unfortunately, Mo spent the better part of his thirteen months in Vietnam being lowered from a helicopter onto a battlefield, triaging, and doing the best he could to save whomever he could.

Mo became a virtual surgeon extraordinaire in his own rights at City ER. His skills with needle and thread were unsurpassed by the residents—and the surgical residents knew it! Most nights when we came in at midnight, they would single Mo out and say, "Ah, thank God you're here, Mo! Thank God!" They had already been up for sixteen hours and were about to go for eight more before their shift was over.

Mo would smile and assure them not to worry, the ER was in good hands. And indeed it was! The surgical resident would then shuffle out of the ER, shoulders hunched, in search of an empty hospital bed. "Remember, Mo, if you get into trouble, I'm just around the corner."

Mo would tap the resident on the shoulder gently. "Worry not…worry not."

When morning arrived, the resident would return looking chipper, holding a cup of coffee, having just had breakfast in the cafeteria. "So, how'd it go, Mo?"

"Like a charm," Mo would say, then unfold the paperwork for what he had done during the night. "The police brought this one in," he'd say. "Found him unconscious by the bus stop. Seems to have had a bit too much to drink, fell and sliced a five-inch gash above his right eye." Mo would give the details of how he had put the man's forehead back together.

"Great, Mo, great!" The resident would say as he signed

off on Mo's surgical wizardry. "What else you got?"

Mo would explain and the resident would put his John Hancock on each sheet. "What would I do without you, Mo, old boy?"

While at City Hospital, I met and became lifelong friends with Sebastian (Sab) Bewig. Sab was a native Baltimorean who had grown up in Dundalk, a working-class neighborhood on the eastern tip of Chesapeake Bay. He worked as the X-ray tech in the ER, the same midnight-to-eight shift as Mo and I.

But Sab took it a step further. He would work from four-to-midnight at Union Memorial Hospital doing X-ray in the ER, then blast across town to start the midnight-to-eight shift at City Hospital, sixteen hours in all. Sab was, and is, an extraordinary photographer. His strategy was to work this grueling sixteen-hour shift for six or seven months, quit both jobs, and head out across the country with his cameras.

Sab was handsome—a consummate lover who had droves of women all the time. With a big, happy laugh he'd tell me, "You won't believe it, but when I got home this morning Elisa stopped by. Wow, what a morning!"

At that time, Mo was dating a wonderful nurse named Karen who worked in the ICU on the same shift. The hospital, being nothing more than a gigantic infirmary for treating the city's indigents, held no awards for sanitation. While working in the ICU, Karen had acquired tuberculosis. My small ratty ER lab, too, was far from clean. It was dotted with splattered blood, sputum, and other bodily fluids on the walls and counters. When I started at City Hospital, I was tested for TB. I was negative. Six months later when I was tested again, I had been infected with TB. Standard treatment for TB back then was to take Isoniazid daily for a year with regular chest X-rays. Isoniazid was hard on the body and no fun, largely due to the slow but persistent growth of the tubercle bacillus it is trying to eliminate. A common side effect is peripheral neuropathy—pain in the extremities such as fingers and hands.

Mo, Karen, Sab, and I partied frequently. Just before I left the insect lab, I started dating Cindy, the daughter of my boss. We'd all get together at one of our apartments with a bushel of clams, crabs, and shrimp. Of the many places I have lived, nowhere can you have a better feast than in Baltimore—dining gloriously like some grand sixteenth century French potentate.

For financial reasons, knowing that my life as a graduate student would be lean, I moved out of my comfortable high-rise apartment and found a place in Highlandtown, a historic working-class neighborhood in east-central Baltimore that consisted of block after block of simple row houses with marble steps that the residents scrubbed white with Ajax every Saturday. The apartment was six blocks from the Hopkins Medical Center, an easy walk.

19

JOHNS HOPKINS UNIVERSITY

I got the letter I had been waiting for. I had been admitted to the PhD program in the Department of Epidemiology at the School of Public Health. When I applied, I had to explain my devasting performance at Circle Campus. I worried greatly that the failed courses from that time would be a total wipe-out for me, but the school seemed to understand. Perhaps I was not the only one they encountered with a similar history; life being as screwed up as it was back then. In any event, I had made it into Hopkins.

I treated myself to a celebration. Around the corner was a neighborhood bar. A very, very simple neighborhood bar. Even more so than any I had known in Chicago. Highlandtown had an infinite number of these—on almost every block you could find one…or two, or three.

The bar was skimpy—a row of stools, a small selection of whiskeys, and one beer on tap: National Bohemian. The one and only local beer drunk in Baltimore—National Boh or Natty Boh to everyone in town. Draft beer at the bar came in a small glass and it cost all of a buck twenty-five. For six or seven dollars, you could get a pretty damn good buzz.

Beer was also sold to locals in stainless steel buckets—a timely tradition my father had told me about that was common in places like Charleroi and other coal-mining towns in Pennsylvania.

In Highlandtown, Pop would send one of his kids with the bucket to fill and bring home.

"Hello, Mr. George," the ten-year-old would pipe, in his high voice as he came into the bar.

"Hey, Sammy."

"Pop needs some beer." He would hand the bucket to George, who would fill it with frothy brew. "Pop says he'll come by later to 'square up', that's what he said."

"Of course, he will. Now don't youse worry about it, Sammy. And tell yer Pop hi. -kay?"

"Thanks, Mr. George. Bye."

"Bye, Sammy."

Sitting at the bar with the stevedores who worked the waterfront, and the steel workers who clocked-in at Bethlehem Steel in Sparrows Point and lived in Highlandtown, I was both elated and frightened about the news from Hopkins. Would I be able to do this, to make it through a degree program at one of the best schools in the country? What if I couldn't? How did this happen, anyway? I ran through the course of events from almost getting drafted to every detail that had brought me here. To this day I still occasionally revisit it. Life is more complex than we know as it plays out one day at a time. It is a castle made of well-trimmed stones laid one upon another. And just like the castle, life's events take shape sometimes with us not even realizing it. Sometimes to our good fortune, sometimes not.

I sat longer than usual at the bar as George doled out boilermakers of shots and beer to the stevedores and steel workers. But it felt good to be there and it brought memories of my days in Chicago, and I greatly appreciated it.

Cindy was elated to hear the news, as was Jim, my former boss at the insect lab. At that time Cindy was spending much of her time at my simple rowhouse apartment. She eventually got a place of her own at 33rd and Charles Streets next to Hopkins Homewood Campus while she went to graduate school for a master's degree at Towson State University. She later went into a PhD program in sociology at Tulane University in New Orleans.

My life became busy as hell while at Hopkins. Classes in epidemiology, immunology, physiology, biochemistry, statistics. I started doing experiments in the lab of Dr. Andrew (Andy) Monjan in the Department of Epidemiology. Learning was exciting, both in lectures and the lab. Andy had a technician who went by the name Skeets. I have no idea where he had acquired the name, but back then, that's who he was. Skeets was a good guy, capable at the bench and lots of fun.

One time while we were working in Andy's lab, we got talking about religion and going to church. Skeets said he had once gone to a Catholic mass with one of his friends when he was a kid. Not being Catholic, he found the whole event interesting, if not a little humorous.

The mass, at that time was said in Latin, as I knew all too well from my days at Maryknoll. Periodically, the priest would turn, face the congregation, spread his arms, and invoke the congregation melodiously with the words, "Dominus Vobiscum." Translated: "May the Lord be With You". But the Skeets rendition was: "Dominoes Nabisco".

Andy was an easy-going mellow person. Consequently, I never felt tension when I was working with him. In fact, unlike most of the faculty at the school, who had degrees in some area of hard science or biomedical research, Andy's PhD was in experimental psychology. It showed in his level-headed approach as a graduate supervisor.

I learned a lot from Andy, but the person who had the greatest impact on me was an immunologist named Gerald (Gerry) Cole, whose office was next to Andy's. Gerry was a shrewd, brilliant scientist with a mind as sharp as any I have known. He had a plush office in the old part of the School of Public Health wood framed windows and doors instead of metal, a set of glass-fronted lawyer-style bookcases along one wall, a leather sofa on the other wall, and an elegant wooden desk. He smoked a pipe, which in 1974 was permitted inside buildings—yes, even in a School of Public Health. He preferred something in the order of a full-bent billiard pipe.

Gerry had recently returned from a sabbatical at The Australia National University in Canberra Australia, where he had worked with an Australian virologist named Peter Doherty and a Swiss scientist named Rolf Zinkernagel. Prior to going to Australia, Gerry and his graduate student, Gene Johnson, made a monumental discovery that demonstrated for the first time how the immune system recognizes virus-infected cells. Unfortunately for Gerry, he and Gene had yet to publish their work. By the time Gerry got to Australia, Peter Doherty and Rolf Zinkernagel had similar findings and had a manuscript in press. Work that eventually garnered a Nobel Prize for the Australian and Swiss scientists.

Upon returning to Hopkins, Gerry's enthusiasm to continue with his work had been partially zapped by what he knew had cost him a great reward. Yet, he was in his office every day, thinking of experiments and chewing on the tip of his pipe.

Hopkins at that time was—and probably is still today—known for its open-ended view of science and research. Students were encouraged to follow their ideas, to let their minds roam. It was unique in that way. And it was a perfect match for me, and for my innate desire to delve into an ocean of possibilities at every turn when it came to research.

There was one big hurdle I needed to get over, however—namely, I had to convince Gerry that my latest brainstorm had merit and that it would work. Convincing Gerry was a formidable task.

I would go to his office to discuss my work, usually to explain something that was not working or not going as anticipated. He would sit at his desk and chew on the stem of his pipe and watch me with a set of brown probing eyes and a frown. After I completed my dialog, he'd think for a second longer, chew on the pipe, then quietly say, "It's bullshit."

Flattened back onto the sofa, aghast, I'd say, "Why, Gerry? What's wrong with it?"

He'd work on his pipe again. Say nothing for a while. Shake his head, and repeat, "It's bullshit, that's why."

Eventually, I'd get up and walk out without an answer.

After doing this many times, I finally mentioned it to Prabhakar, a friend of mine. Prab had started at Hopkins in the same class with me. He was from India and smarter than most of us in the class. One time when we were sitting in the lounge on the first floor, I told Prab about my unproductive discussions with Gerry.

Prab said, "It's easy, John. Don't you see? Gerry wants you to prove to him, intellectually, why you're right and why he's wrong. He wants you to take ownership of your ideas. He doesn't want someone coming in looking for answers or solutions from him."

"Hmm. Think so?"

"I know so. He did it to me until I figured out what he was doing. He still does it each time I go in to talk to him."

"No shit."

"No shit. You need to prove that what you want to do is worth it. *You* need to believe in it. As Gerry sees it, if *you* don't believe it, why the hell should he?"

It was an eureka moment. I could see that Prab was a hundred percent right. Yes, that was what Gerry wanted; I could almost see it in his face each time I had gone in to discuss my work.

From then on, all my many visits to Gerry's office were productive. Most of all, I learned how to think critically as a scientist, something that Hopkins considered necessary from all its students no matter what they were studying. Hopkins wanted to turn out Nobel laureates. But since that rarely happened, at the least it wanted to produce scientists who could think independently.

I had embarked on an area of study to understand the underlying basis for the immune response to *Treponema Pallidum* infection, the bug that causes syphilis in humans. *T. Pallidum* induces a complex immune response, and a complex disease manifestation in humans. During the early 20th century, syphilis was endemic in the US. Research was extensive and the Johns Hopkins School of Medicine and School of Public Health led the field.

Andy arranged for me to work with Dr. Paul Hardy, a pediatrician in the Department of Microbiology at the School of Medicine who had spent his career at Hopkins studying *T. pallidum*. The project was suitable for my interests, and amply challenging, though most of what I learned during that time came from my new productive conversations with Gerry Cole, which occasionally went on for an hour or more.

Paul Hardy's lab consisted of him and his long-time assistant, Ellen Nell. I usually came over about nine in the morning and spent most of the day working quietly at the bench—quite a change from the high-energy days in Andy's lab working with Skeets.

One day early in October of 1978, I decided to make a trip back to see my family in Chicago. I don't think I had been there since Hope and I had trekked out to Baltimore together five years before. I could make the trip to Chicago in a day if I went non-stop. Same thing coming back.

On my return, I drove all night and showed up at my usual time in the Hardy lab. Paul and Ellen were working at the bench. I sat next to them and began with my part of the experiment.

After a few minutes, Paul said, "That was incredible,

wasn't it?"

"What was?" I said,

"About Dan and Ham?"

I had no idea what he was talking about. "Why, what happened?" I asked.

"You didn't hear? They won the Nobel Prize."

"Holy shit!" I think I said.

Daniel Nathans was chair of the department, and Hamilton (Ham) Smith was a professor in the department. They had discovered a group of molecules made by bacteria called restriction enzymes, which were capable of cutting DNA into pieces. But the key here was that they always cut in exactly the same place.

Ham had discovered the enzymes (simultaneously with Werner Arber, a Swiss scientist who shared the Nobel with them that year). Dan Nathans used the enzymes to segment pieces of viral DNA into sizes that could be studied. It was a monumental discovery because it allowed scientists to isolate and sequence entire DNA molecules from viruses and bacteria to gain insights into what made them pathogenic and to understand ways to generate effective vaccines.

As Nobel Prizes go, it was one of the most important awarded for medicine. I remember seeing Dan and Ham walking together to an open-air market a block from the medical center. Daniel Nathans was rather short, and Hamilton Smith was rather tall. You could not miss them as they headed over for their Italian subs at one of the market stalls.

I had now managed to pass all my written exams and two oral qualifying exams, one by the School of Public Health, another by the other schools at Hopkins. Having completed those, I was officially a candidate in the PhD program and needed only to finish my research, write a dissertation, and defend it in yet another oral exam in order to earn my degree.

20

CEDARCROFT AND A TRIP TO MEXICO

In 1978, Skeets bought a three-bedroom row house on Cedarcroft Road on the north end of Baltimore. He used one bedroom for himself and rented one to Geoffrey, a friend of his. Geoff was a Vietnam vet who had a degree in English literature, though by the time he returned from Vietnam his only interest was in riding and fixing motorcycles.

I was still plugging along at Hopkins, but with most of my work completed I was ready to get out of Highlandtown. Skeets let me move into the third bedroom of his place. It was the smallest of the three, but adequate.

At that time, Cindy was spending most weekends with me on Cedarcroft. Parties were a regular event. Thirty or forty friends would show up on Saturdays for a night of music, beer, and fun. Looking back, it had all the electricity of *Party Rock Anthem*, a song and a crazy music video that came out a decade ago but reminded me of our times on Cedarcroft. Of course, we had none of the dancing skills of the Party Rockers, but we sure as hell had the energy. *"Party Rockers in the house tonight. Everybody just have a good time."*

I sold my beloved VW Bug, as faithful as it had been,

and bought a 1967 VW Bus. I don't remember what I paid for it, probably next to nothing. It was in pretty good shape overall, though it had a dull and faded exterior coat of blue paint. Not having enough money for a proper paint job, I bought a can of metallic gold automobile paint and Skeets and I painted the whole thing with brushes, giving it a bright new glow. All things considered, it looked damn good. I dubbed my new vehicle Winnie and painted the name in small blue letters on the back. Thereafter, it was forever known as Winnie.

I removed the back seats and built a platform and plopped down an old double bed mattress that fit perfectly and was just wide enough to sleep three people—cramped, yes, but big enough, nonetheless.

While sitting in the kitchen one morning—myself, Cindy, and Skeets—we came up with the idea of taking Winnie on a trip down to Mexico. Summer was coming, classes were finished, and Skeets had enough vacation time to take a month off. We knew that Andy, being the mellow dude he was, would have no problem with it.

We charted a vague trip that would take about a month, though we agreed that most of the itinerary would be decided once we got to Mexico. We wanted it that way, loose and unpredictable. Why else go? We were not taking a cruise in the Caribbean, after all. And anyway, loose and open-ended fit better with our budgets.

When June arrived, we crammed a few things into backpacks. Skeets brought a small tent knowing that sleeping three abreast in the tight quarters of Winnie would be tough night after night.

During the day, the thin mattress would be rolled up and a canvas director's chair was used for the third rider. It was light and could be set outside in the evening when we needed to unroll the mattress.

We headed out of Baltimore. Everything was going fine for a while. Winnie cruised down I-95 and then across I-10 along the southern states until somewhere down in Mississippi it froze up. We had blown a rod. Oh, Christ, now what? We had only two choices: abort our mission, or find a mechanic who could rebuild the engine, and do it fast. We sure as hell weren't going to stay holed-up in some ratty motel in a sweltering Mississippi coastal town.

We got lucky. There was a mechanic in town who said he could put a rebuilt engine in. He merely had to pull out the one that was in Winnie and trade it for a rebuilt one. It would take him a couple of hours and we'd be on the road by morning. We checked into the cheapest motel in town and by nine o'clock the next morning Winnie and the three of us were off again. I owned one credit card, which I rarely used. But we had no choice, so onto it went the charge of four hundred dollars for Winnie's new engine.

The rest of the trip in the US went quickly. At San

Antonio we took Hwy 57 south to Eagle Pass where we crossed into Piedras Negras, Mexico.

Magically, the world around us changed. The air had the ever-present fragrances that seem to be embedded in every millimeter of the country—dry clay air with wonderful smells from kitchens, cantinas, and cafés, a certain sense of timelessness that is reminiscent of a forgone age. In that way, Mexico never changed.

We passed through the small town of Monclova and continued south until we got to Saltillo where we bought food at the market and made a meal. We were dog-tired, having driven from Mississippi to below the border in Mexico almost non-stop. Rather than sleep in his tent that night, Skeets climbed into Winnie with Cindy and me.

I had attached a sheet of mosquito netting across the back of the bus so we could leave the back door open for ventilation. The netting, fixed to the top on the inside, could be rolled up and down as needed. Until then, we had no actual test to make sure it worked. It seemed perfect…until now, that is.

In the morning Cindy and I felt terrific, well-rested and glad to get a full night's sleep. Skeets, however, was not his usual chipper self.

"Man, did you guys get chewed up by mosquitoes?" he groaned.

We shook our heads, not sure what he was getting at.

And anyway, how could he have been attacked by mosquitoes when we were not?

He pulled up his pants leg and showed us dozens of big mosquito welts. "Well, they chewed the shit out of my leg," he said. "Take a look...all over my foot and ankle."

The mystery became evident soon enough. The mosquito netting on the side where Skeets slept had a six-inch hole exactly where his left foot was.

Cindy roared with laughter. "Thanks, Skeets! You saved us. You became the bait. Why would they go any farther when they could dine on your ankle all night?"

Skeets grinned sarcastically. Of course, we repaired the hole in the netting.

We had little interest in staying in Saltillo which, even with its nice old cathedrals and pretty zocalo, was an industrial city mostly famous for the decorative tiles produced there.

Soon we were on Hwy 57 again, blasting our way south. Winnie performed flawlessly with the rebuilt 1500cc, four-cylinder engine. Being that it was air cooled, we did not have to worry about an overheated radiator in the blistering heat of the Mexican central desert.

We still had no itinerary—it was go-as-you-go. I was interested in stopping in San Luis Potosi to see if it was as I remembered from my visit with Hope. It was a straight shot south of Saltillo about two-hundred and fifty miles, five hours, an easy jaunt for Winnie.

The central desert of Mexico was beautiful in its parched and empty vastness. Dry riverbeds, cloudless skies. It was deadly to be out in it during the day, but inside Winnie even without an AC, the air blowing through the open windows was more than pleasant.

When we got to San Luis Potosi, we wandered around for a while. The city was almost as I remembered from nearly a decade earlier. Evermore charming as one of Mexico's oldest colonial cities, the area was first visited by Cortés in 1522, barely thirty years after Columbus set foot in the new world. The city, which was founded in 1592, teemed with wonderful centuries-old cathedrals and parks and bells that rang gloriously at noon every day for the Angelus and all Sunday morning.

I enjoyed being in San Luis for the short time we were there, but I felt no affiliation to it. Hope's family had been kind and good to me. Quietly, I wished them well, but when we left, I was happy to be gone.

We decided to head west toward the Pacific coast. Exactly where, we weren't sure. We started along a network of large and small roads, weaving our way westward until we arrived at the neighboring villages of Ixtapa and Zihuatanejo. Today, both are bustling resorts; however, in 1978, neither had more than a few small houses with the suggestion of posh new hotels being laid out on the waterfront.

We had a swell meal at a tiny restaurant, but there was very little for us to do in either village. And by now, we were all in desperate need of a bath. The closest we had to that in several days was to pull off the road when one of the transient rain showers dumped a blast of water. We would quickly scramble out of Winnie and rinse off head to foot.

We started south on Hwy 200 that followed close to the Pacific. Thick tropical vegetation brushed the edge of the bumpy road as we moved along. The coast of Zihuatanejo consisted of a series of coves that were protected from the harsh surf.

We parked near a beach that was completely deserted—not a soul in sight. Heading to the water, we noticed a small tidepool about four feet deep where the sea flowed in and out in a slow even motion. Because it was mostly protected from the heavy waves, the temperature was warm and delightful—a wonderful Roman bath made by nature itself.

Taking a saltwater bath may not have been an ideal substitute for the real thing, but we climbed in and lathered up with a bar of soap and doused ourselves in the briny water. When we were finished, we felt clean and refreshed and ready to continue plugging farther down the coast.

We arrived in Acapulco, barely thirty miles south of Zihuatanejo. Although we had little interest in spending time in a big resort that was too glitzy and expensive for our lean pocketbooks, we spent an evening watching the cliff divers scale the rocks and dive gracefully into fifteen feet of water from high up. There was plenty of good restaurants to pick from that fit our budget, so we rented a cheap cabaña for a night, complete with a crude but real shower.

On down Hwy 200, stopping briefly in Puerto Escondido until we reached Puerto Angel, a couple hundred miles north of Guatemala. From there, our journey turned east on Hwy 175 toward Oaxaca. It would take us to our long-awaited goal of San José del Pacifico, a small Indian village nine thousand feet in the sky that was famous for its psychedelic psilocybin mushrooms.

The sun had fallen below the horizon by the time we arrived in San José. The air was chilly. The clouds swooped down and wrapped around the hills and across the small village like swaths of fine linen. We pulled off the road and parked and opened the back of Winnie and prepared to spend the night.

A handful of travelers of all kinds—Americans, Canadians, Europeans, Australians—milled around the mountain village, which in 1978 was little more than a half-dozen adobe houses and one unadorned restaurant-cantina with a dirt floor and a few tables.

I'm not sure how we knew about the famous mushrooms of San José. It's possible one of us had heard about them before we left for our trip, or we had learned from other travelers along the way. In fact, quite a few people who crossed Hwy 175, whether in a car or on the bus that made the trip from Oaxaca to Puerto Angel and back each day, stopped at the hilltop village for a temporary stay.

We hung around Winnie for a while not knowing how to get the mushrooms, but it didn't take long before a local Indian from the village approached us with an offer. He seemed knowledgeable and knew exactly what we would need. He said he would be back in a minute.

When he returned, he had a paper napkin wrapped with exactly enough mushrooms for the three of us and a can of Eagle Brand Sweetened Condensed Milk. Being chewy and earthy and tough on the stomach, the condensed milk made them more palatable. Okay. Simple enough.

It was still early in the evening, but the sun was long gone and darkness surrounded us. We opened the can of condensed milk, doled out portions of mushrooms, looked at each other and with a "why not" and a shrug, started into our psychedelic feast.

As we sat around Winnie, I felt my stomach grumble and growl for ten or fifteen minutes until it finally settled down. We had no idea how to deal with the high—we would each go through it our own way although it did not take long for the buzz to hit. All at once, my mind was "moving low" as the *White Rabbit* had predicted. I remember walking haphazardly around the village, sometimes back to where Winnie was parked, sometimes over to where others were tripping. Everything came alive, not living alive, just alive. In almost every way, it was identical to the high I got from mescaline many years ago sitting on the floor in Bill Putnum's apartment.

I sensed smells I hadn't smelled before, saw radiant splashes of a trillion stars across the sky, listened to the wind as it trickled through the trees of our mountain-top retreat. When I walked, it felt as though the soil beneath my feet was soft and spongy, yet I knew it wasn't. I had a great urge to feel the silence, to let it touch me, to reach out and grab it. Perhaps it was a vestige of the monk-like life at Maryknoll, hidden away in some deep and forgotten recess of my mind, that drew me in that direction. Off and on, I passed Cindy and Skeets—like boats that bobbed and drifted and floated in the gulf stream on a peaceful night.

After a couple of hours, I climbed into the back of Winnie and spent the rest of the night watching an infinite throng of stars that filled the deepest and blackest sky I had ever seen. I felt as though I was out there with the stars, that I was one of the stars suspended in the universe. This went on endlessly. Time had been halted. Back in my days at Bill Putnum's, I had treated myself regularly to acid and mescaline, though I had since given it up. Partly because for me it was something that had to fit into a niche in my life. Now, the mushrooms were perfect for our sojourn across the *Sierra Madre del Sur* in old Mexico.

We all had different experiences that night. When morning arrived, I was quite sure I did not remember all the details of what had happened to me. Some of it had been etch-a-sketched out of my mind almost as soon as it occurred. Yet, I knew that the whole event had been profoundly emotional. Cindy and Skeets returned each with their personal saga.

We all sat on the ground next to Winnie, saying nothing for a long while. Then Cindy said she had been all over the village, had talked to a few people, an Australian couple and three people from Sweden.

Skeets had spent most of the night conversing with a group of Germans, exactly what you would expect of Skeets, the extravert. The person who could always manage to introduce himself to anyone in a simple and sincere way. He said they talked in German most of the night and that he understood everything, though he had never studied German a day in his life and normally could not speak a word of it. Whether that was true or whether it was the mushrooms playing tricks with his head, I had no idea but my preference was to believe it.

Later, we went to the tiny restaurant and had a delicious platter of migas—scrambled eggs with fried tortilla chips, tomatoes, onions, green peppers, slices of avocados, and cups of rich coffee made from beans picked and roasted in the nearby groves. We ate like starving children.

Our ride to Oaxaca took longer than expected. Winnie performed well, but the road weaved up and around and down the hills on a narrow two-lane highway with no shoulder to keep us from tumbling into oblivion.

Oaxaca, one of the most elegant cities in Mexico, was delightful. What's more, we had heard of a camp with all the essential amenities that was out on the edge of town. For a few pesos, we parked Winnie at the camp and from there went into Oaxaca where we ate at a restaurant or went to the market—probably the best one in all of Mexico. We bought shirts and ponchos and brought food back to the camp to prepare meals with.

One morning while sitting next to Winnie eating sweet bread and drinking coffee or cocoa, it was clear our time to return to Baltimore had come. We began out on the twenty-six-hundred-mile trip heading northeast past Mexico City until we reached Hwy 180 on the gulf coast. We stopped only occasionally, once briefly in Tampico before continuing northward. The trip had been euphoric despite periodic visits from Montezuma who assaulted each of us now and then.

Back in Baltimore, our lives quickly returned to normal. Skeets continued working in the lab for Andy. I wrote my dissertation amid daily visits to Gerry Cole's office for episodes of enlightenment. Cindy finished up at Towson State and was preparing to start a PhD program at Tulane in New Orleans.

One morning several weeks after we returned, I was sitting in the kitchen having coffee. Skeets came lumbering in, saying he felt like shit.

As he turned to me, I took one look and said, "Dude…you've got hepatitis!"

"I've got what?"

I looked at his eyes and said, "The whites of your eyes are as yellow as an orange. I mean like jaundice, dude. Like big time. Go upstairs and look in the mirror."

When he came back, he said, "Oh, *shit*…yeah, I got hepatitis, all right."

He called Andy and told him he wouldn't be in, then he drove to the clinic at Hopkins.

There was no question, of course, that he had picked up the Hepatitis-A virus in Mexico from contaminated water or food. And yet, all three of us had the same food, the same water. But, clinically, Hepatitis-A has what is referred to as a case:infection ratio of about 1/3, meaning that the chance of coming down with clinical disease is about one-third. Two-thirds of the people will show no signs or symptoms of disease even though they also were infected. We were a classic example of that. Skeets got hepatitis. Cindy and I came away unscathed. The perfect 1/3 ratio.

I was anxious to finish my degree, but I also was totally burned out. I began hanging out in the evenings at Sebastian's apartment on Lanvale Street in Bolton Hill, drinking beer and listening to jazz.

One night I told Sab, "I don't know man, I'm really bored. Cindy and Skeets and I went to Mexico last summer and, you know, it was absolutely great."

Although Sebastian continued to work in the ERs of various Baltimore hospitals, he was spending more of his time on his photography. I said, "What do you think about us taking trip to Mexico next summer, maybe farther down this time, down into Central America, let's say."

Sab took a hit of beer. I could tell the idea struck a positive chord.

"I don't know if Winnie is really up to it, though," I told Sab. "What about if we do it the old-fashioned way...backpacks and use our thumbs to flag a ride."

And we did. All the next summer we traveled three months in Mexico, Belize, and Guatemala. I took every penny I had, a total of four-hundred and ninety-five dollars for the whole trip.

I won't give you the details of the journey because it's all in my memoir: *To Find: The Search for Meaning in Life on the Gringo Trail*, except to say it was the most transformative experience of my life. We survived a deadly hurricane on the island of *Isla de Mujeres* off the coast of the Yucatan and visited the mystical ruins of the Maya that fill the Peten region of Central America. In Belize, Sebastian met a woman named Donna, who was from New Orleans and was traveling with two of her friends. He stayed in Belize with Donna; I went through Guatemala and then hitch-hiked my way back to the States.

When Sebastian returned, he moved in with Donna in New Orleans for several months. Then one day, they showed up at Skeet's place. Not having anywhere to live in Baltimore, having since given up his apartment in Bolton Hill, Skeets let them rent space in the basement. Now Skeet's original rowhouse had five, and sometimes, six occupants—little by little it was becoming a tenement.

During my time living at Skeet's place in the late 70s, I made my first attempt to write a full-length novel. I had a flimsy idea for a medical/sci-fi tale in which a graduate student working on a doctoral degree in infectious disease immunology (write about what you know...right?) came down with a totally unexplained condition. Her health gradually deteriorated until she ended up in the hospital on oxygen. Little did the medical staff who were treating her know, what she needed was a low mixture of oxygen and a high mixture of carbon dioxide because her body was evolving in a world where levels of carbon dioxide were increasing in the atmosphere due to pollution. In the last chapters, when it became clear she needed carbon dioxide not oxygen, it was too late.

The book, called *La Mariposa*, was truly crappy, and I'm glad I never published it, assuming any credible publisher would even touch it. Not being much of a sci-fi buff, it was the last in that genre I attempted.

Cooking, as much as anything, occupied a lot of the time for most of us at Cedarcroft. Skeets, I think, cut his teeth there and became the culinary aficionado he is today. In his usual persistent manner, I remember him making countless renditions of French onion soup until he succeeded with a damned good version. My explorations included efforts at perfecting a good batch of dark Oaxacan mole, working closely from the recipe Hope had left behind when she departed.

But the real delights coming out of the kitchen were from Donna. Though not yet thirty, she was every bit a gourmet cook in her own right. She often claimed her mother was the real five-star chef of the family. (Behind every good cook is a mother who is a great cook). In any event, a plethora of delectable treats—from sophisticated French cooking to traditional New Orleans Cajun—flowed from the kitchen whenever she set foot inside.

The only one of the five of us who never cooked was Geoffrey. Geoff would come to the house in the evening from his job repairing and rebuilding motorcycles at the shop where he worked, carrying a large twenty-four-piece bucket of Colonel Sander's Extra Crispy Chicken and a two-liter bottle of Coke. Now, of course, it's not to say Geoff ever declined one of the authentically good meals that someone had brewed up.

21

FINISHING AT HOPKINS, OFF TO PENN AND MIT

Trying to get back into the swing of things, I had just enough motivation to finish writing my dissertation and defend it. Anecdotally, one of the signatures on my diploma is that of Donald Henderson, who was the Dean of the School of Public Health the year I graduated.

He had spent more than two decades previously as head of the WHO Smallpox Eradication Program. It had been a massive challenge; however, the last known case of the disease was identified in 1977 in Somalia. Smallpox was officially declared eradicated in 1979. It was the first and so far only time in the history of the world that a major plague had been totally and completely eliminated from the face of the earth.

In September of 1979, the year before I graduated, word was buzzing through the School of Public Health that Dr. Henderson and the WHO would share the Nobel Peace Prize for the extraordinary accomplishment in eradicating smallpox. Cases of champagne had been quietly brought into the school in anticipation of the announcement. Unfortunately, it did not happen; the Peace Prize that year was awarded to Mother Teresa. Even so, I always felt it was too bad the Prize was never awarded for smallpox eradication, as significant as it had been for the world.

In 1980, I accepted a postdoctoral fellowship at the University of Pennsylvania School of Medicine in Philadelphia. I moved into a nice brownstone at 21st and Locust Streets in Center City near Rittenhouse Square.

I quickly made several good friends, including an affable character named Richard O'Sullivan, whom I met at a great pub called *Chaucer's*, two blocks from where I lived. Richard had an infectious personality. He was one of those people you could not help but like. In the spring, we went to Mardi Gras in New Orleans and stayed with Sebastian and Donna at her place in the Uptown District. Richard quickly became the life of every party.

Richard had been applying to medical school but had no success. He had learned of a school in Lille, France that accepted American students. He applied, was accepted, and after two challenging years of medical school classes in French, he transferred to the Medical College of Pennsylvania, which a century previously had started out as the Women's Medical College of Pennsylvania. Founded in 1850, it was one of only two medical schools in the US dedicated solely to training women physicians. In 1970, it began admitting men and the name was changed to the Medical College of Pennsylvania.

Even before going to medical school, Richard had always wanted to be a psychiatrist. After graduation, he applied to residency programs in psychiatry at Johns Hopkins, Yale, and Harvard. He was admitted to all three and opted to train at Harvard. Yet another good example of how perseverance pays off.

I enjoyed Philadelphia a great deal, though unfortunately, my research project was lackluster—it had none of the excitement I got from my work at Hopkins and my interactions with Gerry Cole. In fact, it was Gerry who warned me, in his always direct and unapologetic way, that going to Penn was a bad choice. I went there to join the lab of Neal Nathanson, who had recently moved to Penn from the School of Public Health. Gerry left no mistake in his belief that Neal was a reasonably bright person with little in the way of scientific imagination.

I took on a project in Neal's lab to understand how a certain group of viruses causes neurological disorders that closely mimicked the symptoms of multiple sclerosis. Most of my time was spent working in the lab at Penn, with an occasional trip to Iceland, the only place on the planet that had a colony of sheep susceptible to developing disease following infection with Visna virus, the one we were studying at Penn. It belongs to a virus group generally referred to as slow viruses because it can take up to ten years for infected sheep to come down with symptoms.

Good Lord, it was a lifetime project and I had no intention of spending a lifetime on it. The common joke at the time was that 'there are no slow viruses, only slow virologists'. I felt like a very, very slow virologist thundering across the research landscape with the grace and pace of a brontosaurus. I soon realized that I needed to get myself into something more productive.

One day, Neal said, "John, Stanley Prusiner is in town and he's going to stop by later. We'll all go over to the faculty club for lunch."

We had a great time at lunch. Dr. Prusiner was an effervescent guy who was overflowing with confidence even though he had been fighting an uphill battle trying to convince the scientific community that chronic progressive neurological diseases such as Mad Cow Disease in cattle, and Creutzfeldt-Jakob Disease in humans, were caused by infectious proteins. Prusiner wanted me to join his lab in San Francisco.

The thought was alluring. My project was going nowhere and perhaps this was a good escape valve. After Prusiner left that day, Neal said to me, "You know, don't you, Stanley is a hell of a bright guy. Full of ideas. But the project could easily miss the target all together, leaving you empty handed."

Worse than trying to produce disease in herds of sheep in Iceland, I thought?

The next week, I sent Stanley a gracious letter declining the position in his lab. Stanley, in his undaunting way, went on to successfully prove that his theory was correct, after having isolated what are today referred to as prions. He confirmed their relationship to various chronic neurological diseases, including perhaps Alzheimer's Disease. In 1997, he was awarded the Nobel Prize in Medicine for his groundbreaking work—which, of course, had been ignored for almost three decades.

I am reminded of a great quote by Schopenhauer, which says, "All truth passes through three stages. First, it is ridiculed. Second, it is violently opposed. Third, it is accepted as being self-evident."

While at Penn, I continued to write, usually in the mornings for an hour or so before I went to the lab. I tried a novel but that quickly flopped, so I penned a bunch of short stories and mailed them off to various literary magazines and popular journals. A few were accepted, one of which was an article in a periodical called *World Traveling Magazine* about the trip Sebastian and I had taken to Mexico. It ended up being a feature article with one of Sebastian's photos on the cover.

Two months in Neal's lab was enough for me. I had lost interest in studying infectious diseases from the point of view of the pathogen and was more interested in dissecting out how the body responds to disease, whether due to infection or cancer or from any other cause. Why do some of us get sick while others don't, as was the case with Hepatitis-A when Skeets, Cindy, and I returned from Mexico.

The immune system seemed like a big, complex, enigmatic mass of unexplained contradictions. My interest had turned totally toward immunology. But I needed training, formal training, if I were to dive into a whole new area of biomedical research.

In my rather imitable way, I began searching the world for the best cellular immunologists that I might hook up with. Two names came to the top of the list. One was an older immunologist named Bob Blanden, who was at the John Curtin School of Medical Research in Canberra, the place where Gerry Cole had done a sabbatical just prior to when I started at Hopkins. The other, a similarly important young immunologist named Michael Bevan, was at MIT in Boston.

I sent a letter to each. Bob Blanden wrote back saying they were short of fellowship money, but that he would be happy to sponsor me if I could locate a source of funding. I applied for a postdoctoral fellowship at the Arthritis Foundation.

In the meantime, I stopped in one afternoon to see Peter Doherty (of Zinkernagel and Doherty Nobel Prize fame discussed earlier), who at that time was working at the Wistar Institute, a research facility on the Penn campus. Peter was generous in his appraisal of Blanden, but said, "I'm not sure you should work with Bob. He's a good guy who was once a pretty deep thinker but these days he spends most of his time on the golf course."

Meanwhile, I had received a letter from Michael Bevan, inviting me to Boston for an interview. I took the train from Philadelphia to Boston, spent two days with Bevan and members of his lab, and returned. Three weeks later, on exactly the same day, I got a letter from the Arthritis Foundation approving a three-year fellowship in Australia, and a letter from Bevan saying I could come to his lab. Both requested I let them know in two weeks.

The possibility of going to Australia for three years was tempting but the fear of getting trapped in another go-nowhere project was not. I wrote to Bevan and said I would like to join his lab. Two months later, I was off to Boston.

I leased an apartment on the corner of Anderson and Revere Streets up on Beacon Hill. It was a tiny, charming, second-story, corner flat that looked down on narrow old streets and brick sidewalks in a part of Boston that dated to 1630. I was always charmed by the thought that I was living in a part of Boston that had been settled at a time when Rembrandt was painting in Europe.

From my apartment, it was an easy walk across the

Longfellow Bridge over the Charles River to MIT in Cambridge.

I immediately liked Boston. Having no need for a car when I lived in Philadelphia, and with the availability of decent public transportation, I had sold Winnie with quite bit of sorrow. Boston, with its extensive subway system was perfect for a life without a car.

Mike Bevan's lab was reminiscent of my times at Hopkins working with Gerry Cole. Mike had grown up in Wales, had done his graduate work in London, and had joined the faculty at the Salk Institute in La Jolla, California. While at the Salk, not yet thirty years old, he had done several monumental pieces of work that gave immunologists a window into how the immune system worked in ways no one had envisioned until then. Work that could easily have warranted getting a piece of the Nobel Prize awarded to Rolf Zinkernagel and Peter Doherty in 1997. In fact, either Gerry Cole or Mike Bevan, two people I had the exceptional privilege of working with, could have been co-recipients of the Prize with Zinkernagel and Doherty. I almost felt as though I had jinxed Gerry and Mike.

Mike gave me an excellent project that quickly resulted in a publication in *The Journal of Experimental Medicine*, a top journal for experimental biomedical research. I liked the lab but Mike was definitely unique in the way he interacted with people, especially with graduate students and postdocs. If you were talking with him—talking about an experiment and he didn't like what he was hearing—he merely got up, turned around, and walked away, right in midsentence as you were speaking. Even Gerry would munch on the tip of his pipe for a while and wait to hear what was being said before giving off a signal that the conversation was over. Not Mike, he just grunted and walked off while you were still speaking. After a while you got used to it.

I liked living on Beacon Hill, which afforded easy access to several classic pubs. The two I particularly enjoyed were *The Sevens* on Charles Street, and *The Bull and Finch* on Beacon Street.

It was a simple endeavor to walk a few blocks early in the evening and enjoy a couple pints of Guinness. Both places had loads of charm, classic pub elegance. After I left Boston, *The Bull and Finch* became the prototype of *Cheers*, the bar used in the TV sitcom. Almost immediately, it became a requisite stop on the tourist route—akin to the Old North Church or Bunker Hill. It was never the same place after that.

While in *The Bull and Finch* one night, I met a woman named Susan who lived on Beacon Street in Back Bay. I was thirty-three, she was a few years younger. The bar was crowded so we sat with our pints on the steps that led down into the bar from the doorway and started chatting. She was originally from New Hampshire but worked in Boston and commuted a couple afternoons a week to the University of New Hampshire in Laconia where she was completing a master's degree.

We had good times at her place or mine. My small apartment had a working fireplace, for which I kept an ample supply of wood I bought from a flat-bed truck that came up Beacon Hill every week. We would build a fire in the fireplace and on cold nights when snow fell until morning we slept on cushions from the sofa in front of the fire. It was like something out of a Dickens novel because my corner apartment had an ample view of the red brick sidewalks, narrow streets, and the gas lamps that burned day and night.

Occasionally, we would go to West Dennis on Cape Cod where her family had a house on the ocean side of the cape. Blooms of sea mist were sent into the air from the pounding surf.

We liked to go to Provincetown on the tip of the Cape, especially in the winter when there were only a few people milling around and most of the town was closed but for a few bars, pubs, and restaurants. Provincetown is known for its large, openly gay community. One morning we were having breakfast at a place called The Café Blasé, which was clearly owned and staffed by gays. The chalkboard menu on the wall included all the usual suspects such as eggs, pancakes, French toast, and a couple of different types of cold cereals—one of which was Fruit Loops.

Despite the good times, Susan and I got along about as well as expected given the almost complete Zodiac mismatch, which even though I was not a great believer in, this time it had been pegged spot on. Me being a Virgo and Susan an Aries did not make for a good celestial alignment. She was spontaneous, determined, smart, and most of all impulsive, one who perfectly fit the Aries motto of 'When You Know Yourself, You're Empowered. When You Accept Yourself, You're Invincible'. Being a Virgo, I had always been introspective and a true Virgo perfectionist, one who fit into the motto of 'My Best Can Always Be Better'.

One of the biggest blowouts we had was on a Sunday afternoon, late in the spring of 1982. For no particular reason, I wanted to go to Walden Pond to see where Thoreau had lived, where he had gone, as he put it, "…I went to the woods because I wished to live deliberately, to front only the essential facts of life, and to see if I could not learn what it had to teach, and not, when I came to die, discover that I had not lived."

Susan, who had the only car, was determined to talk me out of it. Not because she had no interest in learning from Thoreau. Quite the contrary, Susan was as much plugged into all things intellectual as I was—more so, possibly. Her argument went something like this:

"*Why…why* do you want to go to *Walden*? It's *packed* with people…tons and tons of them, *everywhere!* You won't see a bloody thing!"

"I don't care, I just want to go. I've never been there."

"It's terrible."

"So what? At least I can say I went to Walden. What's wrong with that?"

Susan, the usually calm, impulsive person growled...and I begged...and we got nowhere...and I never got to Walden on that day or on any other. Yet, the rest of the time we spent together in Boston was fun and adventurous.

One day along about April of 1982, Mike Bevan called me into his office and told me he had taken a job back in San Diego at the Scripps Clinic and Research Foundation, a high-powered research facility. He said I could go with him, or I could stay in Boston at MIT. There were plenty of good laboratories in the Biology Department, which was part of the Center for Cancer Research at MIT.

Good was the understatement. At that time, the department had *five* Nobel laureates. It was without question the most prestigious biology department in the country, probably in the world. Salvador Luria, perhaps the most famous of the five laureates, was the Director of the Cancer Center. Quite a few years previously, he had made a monumental discovery demonstrating that DNA is the molecule that codes for the cell's genetic information. Gobind Khorana, a Pakistani-born scientist, discovered how genetic information makes protein molecules. David Baltimore discovered reverse transcriptase, an enzyme that converts RNA backwards into DNA. Susumu Tonegawa discovered how huge numbers of different antibody molecules are made with only a few genetic templates. Philip Sharp discovered that pieces of DNA called introns, once believed to be useless parts of the genome, play central roles in protein formation.

Any of those laboratories, perhaps with the exception of Dr. Luria's and Dr. Khorana's, both of whom were near retirement, would have been a great choice, and Mike could easily have put in a good word on my behalf.

I liked living in Boston. It is the most European of all US cities and I always had an inclination to live in Europe where food and deep cultural traditions seemed to rule everything in life.

The lure to go to Southern California was quite the opposite, however. I had been to LA a couple of times and had no real desire to live there, but San Diego was a different story—smaller, a community of charming coastal towns and villages. I gave it thought for several days and told Mike I would prefer to work in his lab in San Diego. He was leaving in a few weeks. We agreed I would stay until the end of May when my fellowship ran out.

I told Susan of my decision to go to San Diego. By now life was beginning to coalesce between us. We probably both wondered if there was a future for us, though it was never discussed. The closest we ever got to it was when I asked if she wanted to join me in San Diego. She thought it would be fun but was not able to leave when I did. Perhaps in a month, perhaps two months, sometime in the summer most likely.

22

DEL MAR AND A TREK UP THE AMAZON RIVER

In June, I flew to San Diego and stayed for a couple of weeks at Mike's place until I located an apartment. He had a beautiful house—elegant but nothing really very special by Southern California standards. He once told me, with a certain edge of evident guilt, that he paid more in one month for his mortgage than his parents paid for their entire rowhouse in a coalmining town in Wales where his father worked as a miner.

The first thing I needed when I got to San Diego was a car. I had lived for over three years without one in Philadelphia and Boston, where having a car was more trouble than it was worth, and where public transportation would get you anywhere.

I went to a couple of car dealers in downtown San Diego. Problem was, none of the dealers were willing to sell me a car with little credit and a meager postdoctoral salary.

One afternoon while I was poking around the show room of a Ford dealer, a salesman said, "Here, take a look at this." He led me out to the Previously Owned car lot and showed me a Saab. "We got this in just this week," he said.

"A dentist bought it for his wife, but she didn't like it. She wanted a Ford. Go, figure," he said, with a hardy laugh.

I opened the door and looked inside and checked the odometer. It had almost no miles on it.

"It's practically new. She basically never drove it. And, because it's officially a used car, I can sell it to you with none of the usual rigamarole needed for financing a new car. In fact, if you want it, you can have it for $5,500."

I drove it around the block and up and down the freeway. The price was a fraction of what a new car cost. When I returned, I said, "Let's do it."

I located an apartment at 325½ 8th Street in Del Mar, one of the most enchanting coastal towns in San Diego. Another tiny apartment, about the size of my small Boston place. But what a location! It was on a sandy alley between 7th and 8th Streets. It cost $350 a month to rent; my landlord never raised the rent a penny the entire time I was there.

The apartment was a half block from Camino Del Mar, the main thoroughfare that ran through the village. From the sandy alley where my apartment was, I could look west to the blue respiring Pacific. In the morning or evening, it was simple to go for a run by the sea. I would cross over Camino Del Mar, wind my way down a narrow path called Little Orphan Alley (welcome to Southern California), climb down a set of low cliffs to the beach. The tide in Del Mar was serious, particularly at high tide, and rarely did a day go by when there were not at least a few surfers on the water. They always wore wetsuits because of the chilly Pacific water temperatures.

Standing on the beach watching the surfers one day, I said to one of them as he came out of the water, "So, what's it like out there? Is it cold?"

"Whoa…like ice cream headaches, Dude."

But the best surfing in San Diego was down at Pacific Beach and Ocean Beach or up at Swami's in Escondido. Swami's earned its name from the Self-Realization Fellowship Temple that was and still is situated above the beach. It had been founded in 1920 by Paramahansa Yogananda and has forever been referred to as Swami's by everyone in the area.

My apartment had three rooms: a bedroom, a living room with a small kitchen at one end, and a bathroom. During all the time I lived in Baltimore, Philadelphia, Boston, and Del Mar, I never owned more than one bed, one sofa, a desk and a couple of chairs, some clothes (mostly jeans and a few shirts), underwear and socks, a jacket and a sweater or two.

I frequently think fondly back to those lean times when I consider all the junk, crap, stuff, shit, garbage, waste, rubble, refuse, and clutter I needlessly pack into my life today, somehow convinced it's all necessary, or that it will make me happy, that I can't live without it. And then I eventually throw it out only to buy more junk, crap, stuff, shit, garbage, waste, rubble, refuse, and clutter. We fill up attics and basements and garages with this stuff and build houses with more rooms than any family would ever need or could ever use. And yet some of the most fun moments of my life were when I lived in two small rooms with a small closet for my small wardrobe.

Scripps and the Salk Institute, which were located next to each other, had scores of postdocs in their twenties and thirties. We needed little excuse back then to throw a party, big or small, depending on how many people showed up. Or in the evening, I would stop in at the apartment of Leo Lefrançois and Lynn Puddington who lived a couple blocks away in Del Mar. He was a postdoc in Mike's lab. She was a postdoc at the Salk. Many nights we spent puffing on a hookah or smoking a hash pipe on their back porch with a soft Pacific breeze floating around.

I continued to write, but finally I had something to write about. When I traveled with Sab to Mexico and Central America, I had filled three spiral notebooks with a daily record of everything we did. Lo, I would turn it into a memoir.

Every morning for months I went to the Del Mar Danish Pastry Shop on Camino Del Mar and bought a sweet roll and a cup of coffee and went to the backyard patio and sat under the eucalyptus trees as the sun chased the morning fog from off the ocean. I turned my diary of the trip into a manuscript. Although writing is never easy, the memoir merely required sticking to the details of the daily trek and making sure I got the highs and lows of the journey into it. This I did longhand while at the café. In the evenings I transcribed what I had written into the pages of the memoir using a Smith-Corona manual typewriter.

When the whole episode had finally been recorded, I was pleased with what I had, though I didn't publish it for almost forty years. It was not until my wife read the manuscript and kept prodding me to publish it that I finally did. The final version: *To Find: The Search for Meaning in Life on the Gringo Trail*, became an Amazon bestseller and sold more copies than any of my books to date.

After a couple of years in Del Mar, I had the urge to get away. Living in Camelot was fine, but life in a world where there was little if any rain, zero snow, and perfectly regulated temperatures had become predictable to the point of being boring.

I had heard that it was possible to take a trip up the Amazon River on a cargo boat—no signing up with tourist groups, just go to the Amazon and find a boat. The trick was to go up the river, not down. When the boats went up the river, they hugged the shore as much as possible and the view was always great. Going down the river, boats rode in the middle where the current was strongest and the view of the jungle was too far away to enjoy. The second important point was to start about mid-way up the river. Leticia, Columbia was considered a good place for that.

I got in touch with Sebastian and asked if he was up for an adventure. Stupid question. We laid out a simple itinerary. We would fly to Leticia, first by taking a plane from Los Angeles to Miami (there were no direct flights to Columbia from San Diego or LA), and then to Bogota, Columbia, and from there to Leticia on the Amazon. In Leticia, we would hunt for a cargo boat that was on its way to Iquitos, Peru about four hundred miles up the Amazon. Because there were no roads along the Amazon, cargo boats were required to take on passengers for a nominal fee.

After about twelve hours of connecting flights, we made it to Leticia, an almost non-existent village of a few worn-out wooden huts and dirt roads. Clearly, we needed to get out of Leticia and on the river as soon as possible. There were several barge-like boats along the shore, all of which had destinations upriver. One of them had a load of plywood that filled the hull. Above it was the captain's deck, and behind that and down below was an area where travelers could hang a hammock. It was cramped quarters, to say the least. There was also the top of the boat where we could ride—though weren't really supposed to, but no one stopped us. And it beat being packed inside for what was expected to be a two- or three-day journey.

We climbed on about noon; it was soon quite clear the captain was in no hurry to shove off. In fact, with the exception of a small crew, the boat seemed deserted. A couple of hours later, a barge in front of us fired-up its diesels and started up the river. I was beginning to think we had made a bad choice of boats.

Finally, at last, around nine at night, long after the sun had set, the captain showed up and turned on the engines and little by little aimed the barge onto the Amazon. We were off!

The Amazon River is a unique natural wonder—forty-four hundred miles long, up to three hundred and fifty feet deep, and at its widest point is over a hundred miles across (wider than Lake Michigan). It is the home to three thousand species of fish, many of which are primitive and unique to the river and have yet to be classified. And, of course, one can't forget the pink dolphins that love to follow in the wake of the large boats.

We were provided food: dried fish (piranha, which were plentiful in the Amazon), rice, and water scooped from the river to drink. It wasn't a delicious meal, but the fish was quite good.

Once the boat started, it kept going day and night, no matter how dark. Navigating the river with its submerged logs and tree trunks near shore was a challenge for the captain. One of the crew would stand on the front of the boat with a huge spotlight and call back to the captain if something didn't look good or if he needed to turn left or right to avoid danger. The ever-present hum of the diesel engines continued endlessly. Only once did the boat come to a stop. It happened in the middle of the night when everyone was asleep. I heard the engines wind down and felt the motion of the boat slow as we pulled to shore.

We were technically in Peru, having left Columbia a while back. The boat came to rest at a small military post that had a shack and a couple of people. Two of them came on board and ordered everyone off the boat and onto shore. Most of the people on the boat were locals from Columbia or Peru, with the exception of Sebastian and me and two Europeans.

Soon, we learned what was in store. Everyone was going to get vaccinated against yellow fever virus. They set up a line of people from the boat. Fortunately, Sebastian and I had been vaccinated against yellow fever before we left; we had an International Vaccination Card to prove it. One of the men looked at it, shrugged and nodded in weak approval, and told us to step aside.

Unfortunately for the rest, everyone got vaccinated. Not that getting vaccinated was a bad thing, it was just that it was done by filling a single syringe and going down the line using the *same* needle to vaccinate everyone! When the two Europeans saw this, they refused to get vaccinated. A rather long brouhaha broke out between the Europeans and the Peruvians. In the meantime, the captain was getting anxious to leave. Once it was clear there was an impasse over the vaccine issue, the captain started the diesels and took to the river again, leaving the Europeans behind. It was frightening to see the little hut with a single faint lightbulb in the dark black night shrink smaller and smaller behind us as we left. I wondered what would become of the two who refused to be injected.

On the morning of the third day, we pulled into Iquitos. Though in many ways a poor city, there was an elegance to the central part of it. The city owed much of its storied past to the rubber barons who came there at the end of the nineteenth century when the demand for rubber was great. As portrayed in the classic true story *Fitzcarraldo* by Werner Herzog starring Klaus Kinski, Fitzcarraldo had set out on a near-insane attempt to drag a three-hundred-and-forty-ton steam ship over a jungle ridge that separated two waterways to recover rubber from a dense forest on the far side.

Fitzcarraldo's feat notwithstanding, the barons were known for their extravagant lifestyles that included sending their shirts down the Amazon, across the Atlantic to France, cleaned and pressed in Paris, back across the Atlantic again, and up the Amazon to Iquitos. Still standing in the center of Iquitos was an old opera house of bygone glory from those days.

We rented a room and began searching for someone to take us back into the rain forest, the ultimate goal of our journey. We heard of a person named Freddie Valles, a local resident of Iquitos who had worked as a guide for river and jungle trips which, without someone who knew the dense jungle inside and out, could easily be a death wish. This was not the Appalachian Trail. People who stupidly went into the rain forest on their own were often never heard from again. It was a jungle as formidable as any on the planet due to the assortment of venomous snakes, poisonous frogs, and large cats, not to mention the tribes of Indigenous People, some of whom had little or no prior contact with the outside world.

We met to go over the trip one evening with Freddie at a restaurant where we had cold drinks and ceviche made from Amazon fish, fresh and delicious. Some of the best ceviche I ever had.

Freddie told us about the trip. Besides us, it would include a man and woman from Germany. The entire contingent consisted of the four of us, Freddie, and two porters who he frequently worked with. Although Freddie had been born and raised in Iquitos, his knowledge of the jungle was extensive. He had been a guide for Jacques Cousteau when he did his documentary about the Amazon River and had worked with Werner Herzog on the movie *Fitzcarraldo*.

The trip would take a week. We would start in canoes

up the Rio Napo, a tributary of the Amazon, and then go farther into the jungle on a smaller tributary, eventually taking to the forest on foot. Freddie would bring two shotguns, but we needed to wait a day until he procured shells from a government office—the use of guns in Peru was strictly regulated.

The trip into the jungle was hot, sweaty, and intense. The mosquitoes that everyone assumed would be the biggest problem didn't hold a candle to the ants when it came to tormenting humans. The entire jungle floor was a dense mat of fallen and decaying leaves under which were trillions of ants. One ant having a meal on you inside your pants required immediate attention. I soon learned that the best remedy was to wrap tape around the bottom of my pants the way the porters did.

After a day of going up the Rio Napo followed by a trip up a smaller tributary (the banks of which were adorned with motionless twelve-foot-long crocodiles), we started into the jungle on foot. Freddie led the way, picking the route carefully. There were no paths, or if there were, they had quickly become covered over by the jungle that grew at an astronomical pace.

We hadn't gone far one morning when Freddie stopped and began whistling in a way that sounded more or less like a bird call. I thought that that's what it was—that he was just communicating with a bird given that the jungle was a cacophony of delightful songbird harmonies. This went on for several minutes until out of the jungle came a man, a native of the area. He talked to Freddy briefly and then joined us on our trek deeper into the forest.

His name was Elijo. He was the medicine man from a jungle village, but he didn't like living in the village (too many people, twenty or so). Instead, he spent most of his time alone in the jungle.

It didn't make sense to me. What good was he out in the jungle if a member of his tribe was sick in the village? I asked Freddie this.

"The villagers can communicate with him mentally when they need him. He is always available," Freddie said.

I knew Freddie was stark serious; he wasn't joking. I could tell by the way he said it.

It was a striking revelation. If I learned anything at all from our time on the Amazon River, and back in the rain forest, it was that we in western civilization have lost a great deal of our mental ability to communicate. Sure, we still speak, of course, and now we send messages àla texting and emails by computer. But what we've lost is our capacity to sense, appreciate, interpret, and relate to the world we live in.

Elijo had not lost any of that. In fact, he was as perfectly in touch with his environment as could be. When the villagers needed him, they merely let him know and he returned to help them. And although he may not have been able to perform a triple heart bypass, I have no doubt that much of what he did in treating illnesses came from his vast understanding of the plants that surrounded him. Afterall, so many of our own modern pharmaceuticals are derivatives of plants or plant products—penicillin being a classic example.

We hadn't gone far when Elijo stopped and pulled a couple of large leaves from a tree. He had a pouch with him that had a half-dozen crocodile eggs that he wanted to put aside. He would retrieve them on his way back. He put the eggs in the leaves, folded them, tied them with twine, and hung them from a tree branch to dissuade hungry jungle egg thieves.

On our fourth day, we hadn't gone far when Freddie stopped and said we would be going through a village of Indians. He referred to them several times, saying they were, "Really wild."

I thought he meant this euphemistically given his propensity to use colloquial English. But no. Hardly did he mean that!

We continued on. Soon up ahead I saw an opening in the forest, a few wooden huts with thatched roofs. Freddie told us to stop and wait while he went ahead and talked to the chief, who was dressed in a grass skirt, a grass head band, and a grass breastplate.

Oh, yes, *now* I had a pretty good idea what Freddie was talking about. The women, as with the chief, were dressed in grass skirts naked from the waist up. Freddie and the chief talked in what seemed like a friendly tone, though it was hard to know without knowledge of the language. When Freddy came back, he said the chief told him we could stay a short while, but then we had to move on past the village.

We did not overstay our visit, but while we were there, Freddie showed us the six-foot blowgun that was used to hunt birds and small mammals in the trees. The dart consisted of a thin needlepoint piece of bamboo dipped in curare and wrapped on the back end with a wad of cotton-like material before loading into the blowgun. Curare competitively inhibits acetylcholine binding at neuromuscular junctions, causing paralysis and possibly death by asphyxiation.

For a swap of a cheap Timex wristwatch, the chief was delighted to trade one of the elegant blowguns to Sebastian.

As per request, we did not stay long in the village. The return trek seemed to take longer than expected. We took a separate route that Freddy knew. Elijo left our group and went back to his jungle abode.

On our return, we stopped at a small village on the Rio Napo. In general, the people were not much different from those in Iquitos. We were able to get a good meal of river fish from a restaurant and were able to bathe in the river—

piranha notwithstanding. There is so much for them to dine on in the river, they rarely attack people despite the lore about them.

After the meal, Freddy couldn't wait to treat us to chicha, the home brew made throughout the Amazon region.

Freddy picked up a bowl of chicha and took a sip (I think).

I knew what chicha was. I took the bowl and sipped a little but mostly feigned drinking much of it and then handed it to Sebastian. He took a pretty good slug, swallowed it, and said, "*What-the-fuck-is-that?*"

I explained that chicha was made from yuca roots or corn that was chewed, spit in a bowl, and set aside for several days, saliva and all, until the whole mess had fermented. He was pissed. "You could have told me!" Sab grouched.

Everyone roared.

We made it back to Iquitos and with no desire to ride down the Amazon, we got a ride on a cargo plane with two huge props and flew barely a couple hundred yards above the treetops to Leticia. From there, we retraced our steps back to San Diego.

23

UCSD AND A SECOND ENCOUNTER WITH CARL GALLOWAY

When I returned from the Amazon, I dove into my research project in Mike Bevan's lab at Scripps in La Jolla. My work was going well and I liked the lab, which was filled with a good mix of international students and postdocs.

I continued with my daily routine of running along the beach, sometimes going on weekends down to Black's Beach, the famous nude beach below the high cliffs in La Jolla. After the long six-mile run, I would swim in the chilly Pacific and then bake on the sand *au natural* in the warm sun before suiting up and heading back along the beach to Del Mar.

There were several delightful small cafés and sandwich shops on Camino Del Mar going north to Escondido. One of my favorite places was a café called Coffee-by-the-Sea in the coastal village of Cardiff-by-the-Sea. It had a good selection of pastries and croissants and delicious rich coffee.

I got to know Sally and Danny, who owned the café. Sally was a classic sixties-ish hippy born and raised in Southern California. Danny was from the UK. On weekends, I would work on one of my books, sitting at a table inside the café or on the outdoor deck that viewed the tranquil blue Pacific.

One day after work I drove up to a sandwich shop in Encinitas. As I was waiting for the sandwich, I watched the evening news on a TV mounted on the wall. The news consisted of the usual mix of local and national crap. Then, a story came up and there on the screen was the mug of Carl Galloway—*the* Carl Galloway who had married Hope back in Baltimore pretty quickly after we divorced. It was impossible to mistake him. I heard that they had moved to LA as soon as he finished his residency at the University of Maryland Hospital, but that's all I knew, or cared about.

The story on the screen went on to detail how Dr. Carl Galloway, a Los Angeles physician, was suing CBS News and Dan Rather over a story they had done on *60 Minutes* in 1979 that was titled *It's No Accident*, about physicians who made fraudulent insurance claims by running phony clinics. Apparently, Galloway's name had floated to the top of the list.

I had not seen the *60 Minutes* episode in question, though the news program on the TV in the sandwich shop said Carl was suing for 1.4 million dollars for defamation of character. I felt a certain kind of inner delight in seeing Carl's grim face on the TV screen as he claimed that *60 Minutes* had reduced his medical practice "to a whim", in his words.

Truth be told, I never liked Carl much. Not because he ended up marrying Hope. In fact, it was clear that our marriage would likely not have lasted regardless. She always had a taste for the good life; she realized there would not be much of that in a marriage to a scientist. Rather, I always found something truly disingenuous about Carl.

I had no idea whether Carl had done what *60 Minutes* claimed in their twenty-minute episode, but from what I knew of him, it was fully possible. Carl was a hustler who believed he could get anything he wanted. He rationalized every decision to meet his needs. After Hope and I separated, Carl—who was African American—told me he had long ago decided that he could never marry a white woman, but that he did not consider Hope white because she was Mexican. Have it your way. In fact, Hope had light skin and had come from the upper class of Mexican society. It was how her father had been able to get an excellent education. Her grandfather, a lawyer, had been a leader of the Mexican Revolution of 1920 that brought democracy to the country.

I followed the case on TV and in the papers. As the trial progressed, the judge threw out the 1.4-million-dollar punitive damages part of the suit, which is what Carl claimed he would have lost in his practice from all the bad publicity. This left Carl with a paltry sum of a couple thousand dollars he could still recover from the suit. Worse yet, the jury decided against Carl on all counts. He ended up with nothing from his grandiose legal effort. Only two people have sued *60 Minutes* in all its years: General William Westmoreland and Carl Galloway. The Westmoreland case was settled out of court. Galloway lost as the world watched.

At the end of my year in Mike's lab, I needed to find another place to work. I had zero desire to pack up and move to yet another city. I was as weary of that as I could be so I ended up going to a lab at the University of California San Diego (UCSD) School of Medicine in La Jolla. It turned out to be both a blessing and a curse in the long run.

The lab was run by a gastroenterologist named Dr. Martin Kagnoff. He had little training as a research scientist and it showed in terms of how unfocused his experiments were. Compared to the brilliant minds of Gerry Cole and Mike Bevan, Kagnoff was an intellectual midget. I learned nothing from him directly.

The only benefit for me was that I started a research project that I carried forward for thirty-five years after leaving UCSD. An additional benefit, however, was the spectacular group of international lab partners. Dermot Kelleher was a gastroenterologist from Ireland who went on to hold several deanships at various medical schools. Dominique Kaiserlian and Jean-François Nicolas were from France; each became excellent researchers. Leo Lefrançois made important discoveries in a number of areas of immunology. I had a spectacular research technician named Sandy Sterry from Connecticut, who worked on most of my projects.

As usual, the whole group partied *con mucho gusto* every weekend. We would go to the beach at Torrey Pines at night where there were firepits for cooking. Everyone would bring their own favorite treat for the grill and favorite drinks. Dominique and Jean-François would bring the biggest steaks I had ever seen.

I asked Dominique about that one time. She said, "You know, John (which always sounded like Jean), steak in France ees *very* expensive. You could never afford to buy one like zees one! So, we bought the biggest one they had at Safeway."

I tended to go for fish. Del Mar had an excellent fish monger. Above the counter where whole and filleted fish were spread out on ice was a sign that read: THE FISH YOU BUY TODAY, LAST NIGHT SLEPT IN THE BAY.

The partying would start in the evening and go on almost until the morning.

24

Costa Rica and Nicaragua

My research was going along fine, not because of Kagnoff but in spite of him. In the summer of 1986, I needed a vacation. I began hunting around for an exotic spot. Sebastian would not be able to join me. Donna decided she had enough of Baltimore; they moved to her place in the Uptown District of New Orleans. Sebastian stayed there a while but needing to be closer to the grittier side of life, he got a small flat on St. Anne Street near Royale in the French Quarter.

I decided to spend a couple of weeks in Costa Rica. It was easily accessible by plane from San Diego and for many years I wanted to visit San José—famous for its international expats and known as one of the most progressive countries in Central America. In fact, in 1987 the President of Costa Rica, Oscar Arias Sánchez, was awarded the Nobel Peace Prize for his life-long work fighting for human rights.

I stayed a couple of days in San José, a good place but the hands-down winner of the noisiest city in the world. In so much as San José was on the central mountain range that runs through the country, I planned to go to both the Caribbean and the Pacific sides, neither of which were far away.

There were several ways to get to Limon on the Caribbean, but the train was by far the most exotic method of all. Though barely a hundred miles from San José, the ride slinked down from an altitude of 3,369 feet through dense jungles filled with banana trees and coffee bushes that grew right up next to the train.

Slowly but steadily, the train rolled through one mountain tunnel after another, during which the lights in the train would black out completely, leaving everyone in total darkness. It was a prime setting for thieves who raced through the pitch-black cars grabbing purses and anything of value they could get their hands on.

Limon was an almost degenerate place in which rows of huge turkey buzzards habitually hunched on fences in search of anything edible. I had planned to go down the coast to Cahuita, about thirty miles farther south near the border with Panama, but I would have to wait for the morning bus.

The choices of hotels in Limon were dreadful. I picked what appeared to be the best of the lot and rented a room for the night. It had no windows, one bare electric bulb, and a single almost prison-like metal bed with a two-inch mattress. The walls were made of whitewashed plywood that was so thin it was possible to hear most of what was going on in neighboring rooms. With little to do in Limon, I went to bed early, soon to realize that the main function of the hotel was as a flophouse that rented rooms by the hour.

I was damn glad to see sunlight in the morning. I climbed on the first bus leaving for Cahuita. In less than an hour I was in the coastal village. I checked into a hotel, not great but light years better than the one in Limon and went for a stroll on a beach that was maybe twenty yards wide—on one side, the calm Caribbean, on the other, a thick wall of jungle growth. There was not a soul on the beach.

As I strolled along, I noticed something hanging from a branch of a tree. Wow, a sloth. I moved in to get a photograph when suddenly everything in front of me was trembling to beat hell. I stopped quickly. Not three feet away was a massive six-foot spider web with an orange and black spider bigger than my hand parked in the middle. Seeing that I was about to come headlong into its web, it urgently shook it to warn me off. Neither of us wanted an encounter. The thought of being bound up in a sticky super-sized spider web with a whopping angry spider was overwhelming. I backed off onto the beach.

Coming in my direction was a man and a woman. We stopped and chatted for a moment. I had a Nikon F3 with a 200mm zoom lens on my shoulder. Seeing it, he asked if I was a photographer. To which I aptly denied any serious knowledge of the art.

Later that night, I went to the only place that might be mistaken as a bar in Cahuita. A clapboard building with a dirt floor and crude wooden tables and chairs and good cold beer. I hadn't been there long when the couple I met on the beach came in. His name was Art Dahl; his girlfriend's name was Judy. We all ordered a simple dinner.

He was a photojournalist who had recently completed a photo essay about peacemakers in America, having traveled nine months across thirty-thousand miles through thirty-eight states photographing peacemakers. But these were not your garden variety peacemakers, not as we conventionally think of them. Rather, the fifty-six black and white photographs in Art's exhibit consisted of people who had made peace in their lives or in the lives of others in unique ways. It had a picture, for example, of two North Dakota brothers, both of whom farmed wheat. They had had a dispute many years ago and hadn't talked to each other for many decades, until they finally made peace and put aside their grievances. Art photographed them standing side-by-side outside a large grain silo. There were many other similar photos, each with a brief description of their roles as peacemakers. The exhibit was sponsored by the Greater Boston Physicians for Social Responsibility and had been viewed by more than seventy-three thousand people in Boston and was planning to travel to museums across the US.

Though we had met in the small village of Cahuita down near the border of Panama on the Caribbean side of

Costa Rica, Art had recently come out of Nicaragua where he was doing a photo essay about the Sandinistas.

"But I did one of the dumbest fucking things of my life," he said as we sat in the bleak light of the café. "We had gone into a store, planning to be there just a couple of minutes. When we came out, the side window of the car was smashed, and my two cameras and five lenses were gone. I had shot a dozen rolls of film up until then, but the assignment overall was a total loss. We came down here to Costa Rica to try to recover from the blow."

In fact, it was Art who ultimately talked me into going to Nicaragua. I had been thinking about it for a while but wasn't sure it was such a great idea, though as you may know by now that I am not always given to making wise decisions.

The country had just come through a bloody revolution for independence from the brutal rule of Anastasio Somoza. The Somoza family, initially with help of the US government and later the CIA, had controlled Nicaragua since the 1930s. The government was riddled with corruption. The people were kept poor and uneducated, yet Somoza owned over one-fifth of all profitable land in Nicaragua.

The Sandinista Army, which had started as a rag-tag group of guerrilla fighters in the early 1960s, had gone through one failure after another until Daniel Ortega solidified the group into an effective fighting force that fought Somoza's army village-by-village and house-by-house in bloody battles, finally defeating them in 1979.

Almost immediately, a small group of anti-Sandinista fighters known as Contras battled to overthrow the new Sandinista regime, leading to yet another series of bloody skirmishes throughout the country. The US, fearing the spread of communism in Central America, sent money, equipment, and CIA operatives to Nicaragua to support the Contras. Meanwhile, Ronald Reagan began funneling money to the Contras until between 1982 and 1984 Congress passed the Boland Amendments that prohibited financial support of the Contras.

Not to be deterred by the will of Congress, enter a scheme by Reagan that was as sneaky and devious as ever there was. The US would sell arms to Iran and the Iranian government would pay for them with money that would end up in the hands of the Contras in Nicaragua. It was a plan that was so flagrant, so egregious, it should have resulted in Reagan being impeached.

So now, there I was, sitting in southern Costa Rica, sipping cold beer and hearing about Nicaragua from Art Dahl.

"You know, John, I really think you should go to Nicaragua and take a look around. Get your own idea of what's happening, not the version being peddled in the newspapers up north. The country is as poor as can be, and it's a real eye opener to see it firsthand. Ortega is working with almost nothing."

When I got back to San José, I took the bus to Puntarenas on the Pacific Coast. The village was nice, but the ocean reminded me of the Pacific in Del Mar, so I had no real urge to spend much time there. Rather, I took my backpack and boarded a bus to Nicaragua. A major highway with regular bus service ran up to La Cruz, the last village up near the border with Nicaragua, about a hundred and twenty miles from Puntarenas, perhaps six hours if the usual stops were factored in. I bought a ticket and climbed on the bus…seemed harmless enough.

The bus was mostly full, roughly twenty or so people who were heading to northern Costa Rica, a fact that made me feel better about my decision to go to Nicaragua. As the bus chugged up the highway, however, one by one at each stop in this village or that, people exited the bus until by the time we arrived at the border only one very old lady wrapped in a shawl, and me, remained on the bus. We got off. The old lady walked toward a small border village in Costa Rica.

Shit, now what, I thought.

I could turn around and go back…or…or continue and cross over into Nicaragua. I had gone this far; I decided to go all the way.

I had my passport stamped out of Costa Rica at the small facility on the very edge of the border. When I asked how I could get to Nicaragua, one of the military police merely pointed in a rather stupefied way to a road that led into the jungle. Little did I know there was a three-mile demilitarized zone between the two countries. A No Man's Land that belonged to neither country but was patrolled by both.

All I could do now was start walking into the DMZ. It was late afternoon and I could tell the sun wouldn't last much longer. What's more, the DMZ was itself a foreboding place. There was not a soul on it but me. Just a single narrow road with low jungle growth that enveloped the edge of it. If it was truly three miles long, I calculated I would make it through the DMZ on foot in about an hour—if all went well. It was mid-summer, hotter than hell's shingles with the humidity approaching a hundred percent.

I had walked about a mile, perhaps slightly less, when a jeep came down the road toward me from Nicaragua. I stopped and waited. The vehicle had three Nicaraguan Army men and an ominous-looking machine gun mounted on the back.

"*A donde va?*" the driving said.

"*A Nicaragua,*" I said.

"*Vamanos.*" He pointed to the front fender.

I climbed on. The jeep turned around and headed to Nicaragua. He dropped me off at a large military camp where there was a serious and purposeful immigration station. The majority of the six or eight people ahead of me in line passed through quickly, Nicaraguans coming back from Costa Rica—visiting family, perhaps. I handed my papers to the person checking passports.

"*Americano?* he asked, without looking up.

"*Si…Americano.*"

"*Por qué vienes Nicaragua?*"

"*Como tourista*"

A frown spread across his face; he shook his head as if to say: *No one* comes here as a tourist…do you think I'm stupid? He leafed through my passport, likely trying to see where else I had been, then took his stamp, inked it up, stamped me into the country, handed the passport to me, and waved me on as if wanting nothing to do with *El Loco*.

I looked around for a place to get a room for the night. I was in the middle of a Nicaraguan military base, *not* some lovely resort. There was nowhere to stay. I enquired about a bus to Managua but quickly learned that I was stranded. No buses ran up to Managua, and I could not stay where I was. One other person was in the same pickle. He was either European or Canadian—I don't recall.

As I've learned from being in these situations more than once, sooner or later a solution will present itself. This time it was in the form of a truck that was going to Managua. The driver agreed to let us ride in the back. The truck was a simple, worn-out, grey affair about the size of a medium U-Haul with no back door or back gate. Just a heavy tarp tied at the side.

He said he would take us to Managua. He didn't know how long it would take. Five hours, six maybe. He had a business of some kind that involved delivering fruit and other food to parts of Nicaragua. Though the truck was mostly empty, he would be making several stops to load up along the way.

He gave us a few very important instructions. One, the truck would be stopped at checkpoints periodically. There was no telling where this would be since they were randomly moved from spot to spot. The truck would be inspected, but usually only casually. Maybe a look in the back. Maybe not even that. Two, when we were stopped, we were to climb under a tarp that was in the back of the truck. "Get under and don't move. Keep still...*totally!* If discovered, get out and do what you're told." Three, we were not to get on the truck while at the military base. The driver would give us a thirty-minute lead to walk away from the base. Then he would pick us up down the road. The people at the base were no idiots. They knew exactly what would happen, but this way they could pretend they were oblivious to it if questioned.

We did as he said and started down the road until it curved around a bend. Soon, the truck came by. We climbed on back and off he went down a jagged and rutted road.

Just as we had been forewarned, the truck rolled to a stop at one check point after another every twenty or thirty minutes. And, exactly as described, someone from the check point came to the back of the truck with the driver, who explained where he was going and what he was doing. With little ado more than that, we were off again down the road.

The view from the back of the truck was nice despite being a trip that crossed land scarred by decades of war. The road followed the edge of Lake Nicaragua for twenty miles or so, then swung westward for a while, then made a right turn and arrived at Granada on the top of Lake Nicaragua some four hours later. The city, a beautiful colonial town, was founded by Francisco Hernández Córdoba in 1524. Prior to that it had been a thriving city of Indigenous People for hundreds of years.

The driver stopped in Granada and put a small batch of fresh fruit and vegetables on the truck. He said he would be back soon, which stretched into more than an hour. He went into a house and apparently had a leisurely dinner. Rather than sit in the truck, we got out and wandered a short distance up and down the street where I witnessed something unnerving and shocking. On the front of almost every house was a brass plate with the name of one, two, sometimes three people, always never more than in their early twenties, a few in their teens, who had given their life in the fight for freedom against Somoza. It was a moving and humbling sight to see.

In time we were going up the road again. More check points, more rutted roads. The sun had long since set and we seemed to be creeping at a snail's pace. At around eight o'clock, the truck pulled into the city of Managua, an entire city with virtually no light but for the headlights of the occasional cars going up and down the streets. Managua was so poor, so crippled by the constant battles with the Contras and other forms of external trouble, that it could not afford to light the streetlamps. Every inch of the big city was filled with utter darkness.

We hadn't gone far before the driver pulled over and told us it was the end of the line for him. I enquired about a place to stay for the night. He said he knew of no hotels in Managua—thus leaving me with another worrisome situation. Fortunately, there was a household that, as he knew it, rented rooms. He drove us there, merely a few blocks away.

I went inside a small, unbelievably bare house. The woman who greeted me at the door confirmed what the driver had said. We could use the empty bedrooms. The fee was embarrassingly small. I took up the offer. My traveling companion had no desire to stay. He decided to scour the city for a real hotel. Not me. I was beat to death. I paid the fare, went to the room, and fell on the bed, totally blasted after a day that started out on a sunny beach in Costa Rica and ended in blacked-out Managua.

In the morning, I headed into the city to find a hotel, hopefully one with better accommodation.

Managua was a charming but impoverished city still stinging from the effects of years of war. It had most of the usual stores, shops, restaurants, cafés, and cantinas one finds in any large Latin-American city, but there was a wrenching soulful feeling of desperation that permeated everything.

After hunting around, I heard of a small motel-like place in the heart of the city that rented rooms. I grabbed a taxi in the zocalo. The driver knew right away where it was, which by itself, was a good sign.

I got a room, sparse and plain but clean, with a small patio that opened to a grassy courtyard. I purchased a pack of Nicaraguan Córdobas at a bank. The only form of currency used in the country was the Córdoba or the American dollar. Costa Rican Colóns were useless.

In all, I stayed four days in Managua, having realized that there was little to do but walk the streets or hang out at one of the cafés drinking cold beer or rich Nicaraguan coffee.

I was careful—extremely careful—when photographing the city and the life of the people, something that had been one of my goals for the trip. But it became immediately obvious that anyone with a US passport, or who looked and talked like an American, was assumed to be a mole for the CIA. Art Dahl could get away with it given his credentials as a legitimate photojournalist.

What's more, this was 1986, a time before instant communication. I hadn't mentioned my plans to trek off to Costa Rica (and Nicaragua) to more than a few people, maybe only to Karen McAlpine, whom I was dating at the time, and some of my lab cohorts. I had not mentioned it to my parents—they would have thought I had lost more than a few marbles.

I made up my mind to return to Costa Rica the next day. I learned, to my surprise, that there was a daily bus that ran from Managua to the border near Costa Rica.

The following morning, I sat in a café near the motel drinking *café con leche* as had become my routine for the past several days. The café was nearly empty but for a man and woman sitting nearby. Finally, perhaps out of considerable curiosity, the man introduced himself. He was an American; the woman, his wife, was Nicaraguan. Both, somewhere in their thirties.

"*Buenos días*," he said. "What brings you to lovely Managua?"

I wasn't sure if he was serious or not. "Oh, just looking around…you know, tourist junk." I pointed to the camera bag next to me.

The woman nodded. She explained that they had been living in Nicaragua for a while.

"And where to today, if I may ask?" the man said.

"Back to Costa Rica. That was my original destination when I left California, then I decided to make a trip up here. Anyway, I'll be climbing on the bus that goes to the border."

The man's eyes lit up. "Well…you might have a little trouble doing that today," he said.

"Oh…why?"

"The border is closed."

"Say again?"

"The border is closed. We heard it on the radio this morning."

I wanted to laugh but couldn't. "Closed?"

"Yes, it happens quite a lot. The Nicaraguans get pissed, or sometimes the Costa Ricans get pissed, and they just close the border for a while."

I slumped down and stared across the room. "For how long?" I said, returning to the man.

"Your guess," he replied, with a shrug. "One day, two days, three days…who knows?"

I moaned.

"It happens all the time," the woman said.

"Oh, shit…now what?"

"The only way out today is to fly out. That's all you can do. There is one flight a day to Costa Rica." He looked at his watch. "But it's leaving soon. In about an hour. If you want to get on it, you need to get to the airport quick."

"*Gratias, gratias*," I said, dumping a handful of Córdobas on the table and grabbing my camera and pack.

"Get a taxi to the airport. *Adiós* and have a good trip," he called, with a friendly smile.

I flagged the first taxi I saw. We were at the airport in less than ten minutes. Small, but like any airport anywhere. Just as the man at the café had said, a flight was posted to leave for San José. I rushed to the ticket counter. The woman at the counter spoke good English.

"A ticket to San José," I implored.

"Ninety dollars," she said.

A lot of money, I thought, for a twenty-minute flight. But no matter, I needed to be on the plane. I pulled out a roll of Córdobas.

"Oh no, Sir. Oh no, the ticket must be paid in dollars. US dollars. Only dollars. Nothing else."

No problem, I thought. I took out my folder of traveler's cheques.

Seeing this, she repeated, "No, only in dollars. Only dollar bills we take."

"But these are dollars."

"We must have cash. Dollar bills."

"Where can I get the cheques cashed?"

"In a bank."

I knew that was hopeless. "It will take a long time to do that," I said urgently.

"Yes, and the plane is leaving soon," she said, looking sympathetically at me.

Now, for once, I was at an impasse.

"But…you can go out of the airport and around the corner where you will find a man who will exchange the cheques for you. If you go quickly."

I raced out of the terminal. Sure enough, a man sat on a small stool behind a cheap card table. Coins and bills stacked on top of the table. I told him my predicament and peeled off two fifty-dollar cheques. He handed me the dollars. I gave him ten for his services and raced back inside and handed the money to the ticket agent. She printed a ticket. I boarded the plane as they were about to close the door. Before I was in my seat, the Boeing 737 was moving down the taxiway for the runway. I had made it with barely a minute to spare.

The entire flight took hardly twenty minutes—up then down, two hundred and thirteen miles.

I stayed another two days in San José. The same noisy, busy place as when I was there the first time, but now I was more delighted than ever to sit in the bars and outdoor cafés and chat with the collection of international expats over beer and whiskey and tequila. Many of them had also made a trip to Nicaragua at one time or other. Overall, the expats were an enlightened bunch, if perhaps strongly opinionated, which never bothered me so long as people knew what they were talking about. They did.

I returned to California. Shortly after, I got a letter from Art Dahl. It was accompanied by a poster of his exhibit, which to this day hangs in my office more than forty years later. In the letter, he wanted to know if I could put in a word with the director of the San Diego Museum of Photographic Arts, whom I casually knew, about an exhibit:

"Dear John,

I hope you like the poster. The show was a tremendous success and 12 -14 other PSR chapters want it (not San Diego so far). We're going to Washington next week to the National Office to work on a touring schedule. Maybe Ullman's place would be a good site. He and I were together in Yosemite the last year (1981) that Ansel ran his 4-8 week workshops.

Best Wishes,
Art"

25

OUT OF CALIFORNIA AND INTO OKLAHOMA

In *The Grapes of Wrath*, Tom Joad migrated with his family from Oklahoma to California in search of work. I, as it were, left the good life in California and moved to Oklahoma in search of work.

My days in Kagnoff's lab were getting worse and worse. I did, however, manage to publish a superb paper in *The Journal of Experimental Medicine*. The problem, as Kagnoff saw it, was that I had not included him as an author.

I had grown up, scientifically, with excellent mentors in the form of Gerry Cole, Neal Nathanson, and Mike Bevan who knew, and practiced, the fundamental rule that scientists do not randomly slap the name of another scientist as an author on a paper if they had not made a substantial contribution to it—at least intellectually—if not at the bench.

Kagnoff had done neither. He had a reputation as being a scientific leech, although he had mostly left me alone, until now.

When he found out about the paper (actually, I gave him a copy of the galley proofs that were sent to the authors by the journal before it appeared in press), he blew a fuse—

and I mean a damn, fucking, big one. Afterall, this was how he had amassed his publication record, not by the grit of planning and designing and executing experiments. Anecdotally, all my scientific life, I have been reminded of the comment of Richard Gershon, a truly great and inspirational immunologist, who said, "To be a good scientist, you have to think until it hurts, and then you have to think through the pain." Kagnoff had never done any of that.

In truth, I was not officially in Kagnoff's lab, but by agreement I was using some of his space at UCSD. When he found out about the paper, he did the one thing he knew would screw me the worst. He took away the space he had lent me.

There I was with a thriving research project funded by the National Institutes of Health and an extraordinary research technician, Sandy Sterry, but with no place to work. I was scientifically homeless.

There was a famous immunologist named Richard (Dick) Dutton whose lab was in a building just across from where I worked. I walked over and told Dick my dilemma. He agreed to let me and Sandy use a small but adequate chunk of his bench space. Dutton wasn't worried about repercussions from Kagnoff. His standing in the immunology community was something Kagnoff could only dream of.

I needed to start looking for a permanent position since it was clear I would not be able to work in the small area

Dick was offering, though he never said anything to suggest I leave.

I looked through the back pages of *Nature* and *Science* journals where the good positions were posted from schools that had openings. I hoped I might find something back in Boston. Southern California was all right but living in Camelot, as the locals liked to call it, got tiresome with its perfect weather, perfect people, perfect lifestyle. What's more, each year it became more crowded. More cars on the freeways, more people at the beaches, more bumper stickers that said: *Welcome to California, Now Go Home*.

I applied for two Assistant Professor positions. One at the University of Indiana Medical School in Indianapolis. The other at the University of Tulsa in Tulsa, Oklahoma. I got an offer from both but, being tired of the rigid demands of medical schools and high-powered research institutes, I accepted the position in Tulsa. Perhaps a plain old biology department was what I needed.

I moved quickly to Tulsa. I had what little furniture I owned shipped out and drove my Saab across the California desert and through Arizona and New Mexico into Oklahoma. Never having been to Oklahoma, I had no idea what to expect. Getting used to the southern slang was fine, and the version in Oklahoma was not nearly as bad as what I remembered from places like Alabama and South Carolina. It had a certain melodious ring to it.

There were a few words, however, that took me a minute or so to translate. In Tulsa, at least, the word for deli was delly. I saw it written on grocery store windows but had no idea what it was. And I wasn't sure for quite a while what the hell a bokay was until I saw a bunch of flowers in a store next to a bokay sign and figured out it was Okie for bouquet. And, of course, in Tulsa your local bar advertised draw beer on signs out front, which I learned was Okie for draught beer. Oh well.

Beyond that, I managed to translate the rest quite easily. However, I do remember once when I went to have some blood work done, the person taking the blood said, "Put your pepper down there."

I stared at her for a second, not knowing what she wanted.

A second time she said, "Put your pepper down there."

Again, I stared.

Finally, she grabbed the paper out of my hand and slapped it on the counter. Now I knew.

But Okies had as much trouble understanding me as I did them. More than once, a student came up to me after a lecture and, with a rather beguiling look, asked, "So...where are you from, anyway?"

Touché.

I set up my lab at Tulsa quickly. They gave me good facilities and ample lab space of my own. No prick like

Kagnoff to answer to. My teaching load was meager. Since I had never done much teaching until then, it was a *big* adjustment. I truly believe that good teachers are born, not made. Some people love doing it and have a knack for being good at it. I always tried to do the best I could in the classroom, but even after many decades it was clear I would never master the art of teaching.

I rented a house less than a mile from the university. I was nearly forty and had yet to own a house of my own, partly due to all the moving around I had done in the past ten years. Times are different now. I get the feeling that owning a home today is a big goal for people in their twenties. Of course, when I was in my twenties, I was getting stoned, tripping on acid and mescaline, and protesting a war. Owning a home was way down on my priority list.

The faculty in the Department of Biology at Tulsa turned out to be a great bunch and a lot of fun to be with. Unlike medical schools, where almost everyone worked on something close to what I did, the Biology Department was a diverse lot that included entomologists, ecologists, herpetologists, geneticists, botanists, ornithologists, molecular biologists, and others.

It was great fun interacting with people who were experts in reptiles or birds, especially on Friday afternoons at the Beer-of-the-Week-Club meeting—a tradition that had been going on in the department for quite a while. Each week one of us would host the end-of-week retreat at their house by buying a case or two of imported beer, which always varied from week to week.

The first addition to my lab was Lee Mosley, who started as a technician and then entered the PhD program and conducted his graduate work in my lab. Lee was a bright person who did first-class research in developmental T cell biology and went on to a stellar career as an independent NIH-funded investigator.

Meanwhile, my lab had turned into an international affair consisting of Jin, a Chinese doctoral student, Mawieh, a Jordanian doctoral student (who actually was from a Palestinian family that had been displaced years ago when they had been uprooted in Jerusalem), and Umit, a Turkish postdoc. My experiments in the lab were done by a Texan/Okie named Mike.

Everyone got along well except when Mike stirred the pot, which he did often and which greatly pissed me off, not to mention the way it caused a high level of turbulence in the lab.

Even so, Mike was an exceptional, if rather weird, research tech. He was like Radar O'Reilly in the movie *MASH*. At our twice weekly lab meetings we would go around the table and one-by-one each person would review what they were working on and what they had recently done. I would tell them how they might tweak their experiments if things weren't going well.

When it was Mike's turn, I would say, "Okay, Mike, what I want you to do—"

"I already did that," he'd say.

I'd look at him, befuddled, and say, "You did?"

"Uh-huh," he'd dryly utter.

"Hmm. Okay, then what you need to do now is—"

"I started that yesterday," he'd reply.

"You did? How did you know I wanted you to—"

"I knew," he would succinctly reply, looking bored, and then add, "And I also started the…" and he would tell me he had begun to clone a gene I was thinking (thinking) about getting to.

Jin and Mawieh worked hard and both finished with very respectable PhD dissertations. Mawieh returned to Jordan. Jin left biology and got a second advanced degree in computer science because it didn't require writing English, something she always struggled with.

Umit, who spent a couple of years in my lab, turned out several first-rate papers, though of all the people in the group he had the most unconventional work routine. He would arrive in the lab at ten or eleven in the morning and, being enormously gregarious, he would spend his day wandering around the department hob-knobbing with graduate students and postdocs in other labs. Eventually, when everyone had left for the day, he would begin his experiments, work until two or three in the morning, then head home and get some sleep. He had a wife and a wonderful young child that he would spend time with before coming to the lab and start over again.

In Tulsa, I returned to writing again. The first was a novel of literary fiction titled, *Frankie Jones*. It had autobiographical elements but was not truly an autobiography. I had an urge to write something heartfelt. I had recently read several books that were awe-inspiring when it came to writing. Two were by Jack Kerouac, *The Town and the City*, and *On the Road*. The other was what I have considered to be one of the best books of the twentieth century, *Barbary Shore* by Norman Mailer.

I learned from all three books that to write good fiction it's necessary to open your soul and pour out everything inside. The emotions need to be intense and penetrating. Yet, it is important to adhere to the fundamental tenet of good fiction writing, that is, to write sentiment, *not* sentimentality. Putting sentimentality into writing is easy, but cheap and ineffective. As Flannery O'Connor said, sentimentality is a "distortion of sentiment".

So, aware of that, I tried hard to scrub my writing of sentimentality. *Frankie Jones* had not been a financial success by any stretch, but it pulled in a few good reviews, including one from The US Review of Books:

"...*echoes of Hemingway's* The Sun Also Rises *linger in the* white spaces of Klein's beguiling novel...Klein has written a novel one doesn't find anymore—as much exploration as exposition, it often raises unanswerable questions. His prose is lyrical and frequently sings, in a minor key, of things we too often take for granted. Courageously non-genre, this novel is for people who love language, appreciate insightful perceptions of the human condition, and accept the realization that nothing really ends as long as life goes on."

I also tried my hand at a theatrical play. I had long wanted to write something about the Vietnam War, though not having been there, I had no firsthand experiences I could draw from. Instead, I framed the play, titled *Teach Your Children*, around a family of five: two parents who were of the World War Two generation, and three siblings: a son who was a decorated Vietnam veteran, a son who had managed to avoid the draft by going to medical school, and a daughter who had actively protested the war. What little I knew about script writing was that it had to have a beginning, middle, and end (like all forms of creative writing), but most importantly, there had to be a crisis and a resolution of the crisis. That occurred when the father, a World War Two veteran and his Vietnam veteran son got into an argument over the validity of the Vietnam War.

The play was never officially performed except as a reader's theater by the Theater Department at the University of Tulsa. This consisted of having actors read the play on the stage from the script, principally so the playwright can hear how it sounds, which, unlike writing a book is necessary in the case of a play. The playwright also got direct feedback from the audience.

Today, the script sits in a stack of other crud on my desk.

The person living in the house next to me was a professor of Spanish Literature at the university. Her name was Jane Ackerman. Our yards were separated by a four-foot-high chain link fence. We would talk across the fence when we were coming and going, and little by little we would sit in my back patio with a glass of beer or a cup of wine.

Like me, Jane had been married previously, in her case to a medical student at Northwestern Medical School. After he graduated, they moved to Alaska where he worked on an Indian reservation. It was part of the program he signed up for in medical school. The government paid his tuition and in return he was required to practice medicine for four years in some area where there was a shortage of physicians. The choice of where to go was up to the physician. In the case of Jane's husband, he chose to work on an Indian reservation in Alaska. Jane stayed for three years, then got divorced. I'm not sure why. Her ex-husband never left Alaska and more than twenty years later, he still works on the reservation.

The program Jane's husband had been part of was a good one, but it was eventually shut down as more and more medical students said to the government, "Hey, fuck you," and took off for lucrative practices somewhere instead of doing their required community service. It's pretty damn hard to force someone to work in an inner-city ghetto when they refuse to no matter what contractual agreement they had inked their name on.

While in Tulsa, I got a dalmatian, which I named Pablo. He was great fun. We would go for runs in the park together. One day, I took him to the animal hospital to get his claws clipped. Weirdly, when I got him back, they had put pink nail polish on this front claws. Don't ask why. In any event, when Jane saw it from across the fence, she thought I had done it, though she didn't enquire until she finally mustered the courage to ask a few days later.

After a year or so, we moved into a house together. It had a pool and a nice big yard for Pablo and Jane's two cats—Larry and Pansy—to snoop around in. And plenty of room for a multitude of tomato plants, which grew extremely well in the hot dry climate. We stayed about a year and then bought a house—my very first home purchase.

Although, overall, Jane and I got along reasonably well, in many ways we were oil and water. Sort of a 'you say po-ta-to, I say po-tah-to; you say to-ma-to, I say to-mah-to' kind of thing. A day without an argument was a day without sunshine. Even being the serious perfectionist I am, I don't like arguing. Especially over nonsense. And that's what most of our arguments were over…nonsense. It's a waste of time and exhausting. Regardless, in 1995, Jane and I got married, this time not by a Justice of the Peace, but in a slightly more formal wedding at our house.

Our differences translated into almost everything we did, even down to our choices of vacation spots. My ideal vacation was sitting in a beach chair on the sand on a quiet Caribbean island, snorkeling, dining at a fine French restaurant. Jane's preference was to slog up and down mountain trails in Colorado, something I always disliked. Mountains made me feel claustrophobic, as if I were being squeezed in by the high hills on all sides of me. Nonetheless, we did manage to get to a few good islands—notably, St. Barts, Anguilla, St. Maarten, Turks and Caicos, Aruba, and a few others.

We also had great dinner parties back then, the first time I had ever been to an actual dinner party. I always thought such things would be horribly dull and dreary; they were anything but. Besides Jane and me, they usually consisted of three or four other couples—mostly faculty and spouse from various liberal arts departments. Sometimes a scholar of Western America history, or an archologist of Middle East antiquity, or a painter or art historian from the art department. The parties were fun and enlightening events that went on for hours with discussions that moved casually through a multitude of topics amid good food and wine. No one was there to give an academic lecture to the rest of us, or to prove how cool and famous and sharp they were. I enjoyed every dinner party I went to.

Yet, little by little, life between Jane and me deteriorated. I had enough of the useless arguments. The problem, however, was that they were impossible to stop unilaterally. If someone is continually lobbing hand grenades in your direction, there is little you can do to stop it. I remember Jane once telling me her parents battled with each other almost nightly. Whether we think so or not, we are too often imprinted with behaviors we experienced or witnessed as a child. In fact, it may have been part of the reason why I never wanted to have children of my own. I was never convinced that frightening 'clones' of me on this planet would be such a wonderful thing.

The decision to separate came abruptly, and it wasn't easy on my psyche. Now I had struck out twice: once with Hope and now with Jane. After the divorce, I knew I needed to get out of Tulsa and try to make a fresh start. I was at a low point in my life and to make it worse, Pablo, my loyal companion for thirteen years was sick and had to be put down.

26

HOUSTON
OUT OF DARKNESS AND INTO LIGHT

Oklahoma had been all right, or as the slogan on the license plates read when I got there—*Oklahoma is OK*, which was eventually replaced when Okies began to complain about the ho-hum statement, cute and well intentioned as it might have been. Life had bottomed out in Oklahoma; I needed a change of scenery.

I started once again to look for a position. After interviewing at several places, the best offer came from the University of Texas Health Science Center at Houston—a massive complex of twenty-two hospitals, the largest medical center in the world. Including the MD Anderson Cancer Center, a hundred and ten thousand employees came and went each day to the Medical Center. I accepted a position in 2000.

With little else to do, I spent most of my time setting up my lab. The administration had been generous to me, having given me plenty of space and a large and roomy office. In the evenings, I went to one of the almost infinite numbers of great restaurants the city had to offer. I knew I had to rebuild my life—but knowing it and doing it were two different things.

One afternoon I was working in my office when I got a call from Dr. Karen Storthz, the Associate Dean for Research, the person who was mostly responsible for recruiting me to the Medical Center.

She said, "John, when you've got a minute, stop down at my office."

I went to the first floor and knocked on her door.

"Oh, hi John. Come in," she said. She told me that Dr. Ron Johnson, the Dean of the School who had actually made the decision to hire me, would be getting in touch with me. He had a special request.

Sure enough, a couple of hours later I got a call from Dr. Johnson.

"Hey, how are you doing, John?" he said in his usual ebullient manner.

"I'm doing fine, Ron. Thanks."

"Everything okay in the lab?"

"Oh, yeah, sure. Great."

"Got a question," he said, in his typical staccato way of speaking.

"Shoot."

It turned out that Sandra, Dean Johnson's girlfriend, worked in a dental office with a person named Jeanne, who a little while ago had gotten out of a relationship.

"I want you to meet someone," Ron Johnson said.

Oh God, I thought. Not the dreaded blind date! But I figured, well okay. Why not. My days to that point had been a bit dreary.

"I've got some tickets to the Impressionist exhibit that's at the Houston Museum of Fine Arts now," Ron said. "Will this weekend be all right?"

"Sure," I replied. I am not sure how enthused I sounded, but something told me to go ahead with it.

On Saturday evening, we went to the exhibit. Room after room of works by the Impressionists. Afterwards, pizza at a local restaurant. I had a great time. I hoped Jeanne had also. At the end of the evening when I asked if she would be interested in going out again, she said she would. I was hoping she meant it.

But she did. A few nights later we went to a small romantic Italian restaurant. We were the last people to leave. From then on, we saw each other regularly.

Jeanne had a son named Jordan, who at that time was in seventh grade. A year or so later, I bought a small but elegant bungalow near the Medical Center and the three of us moved in. It took some transitioning for me—to say the least—having never had children of my own, but given that I loved to cook, I was happy to come up with something delicious at the end of the day.

Meanwhile, my research had moved into an area that

was a spinoff from what I had been studying for many years. I became interested in the gene that makes thyroid stimulating hormone (TSH), which is produced by the anterior pituitary and regulates the release of two hormones from the thyroid that, in turn, control essentially all aspects of human growth, behavior, metabolism, and cognition.

It had been known for several years that TSH is made by the cells of the immune system; however, the purpose of that was a mystery.

A graduate student in my lab determined that the type of TSH made by the immune system was unique from the conventional type made by the pituitary. Different forms of genes are called isoforms. The isoform of TSH that we identified in the immune system was the first of its kind to be characterized. Moreover, it appeared to be linked to autoimmune thyroid diseases such as Graves' disease and Hashimoto's disease. Rather quickly, other investigators found that it was used in bone development and played a role in osteoporosis. I applied for and received several grants from the National Institutes of Health to study the isoform.

As always, I was lucky to locate a terrific and very smart research technician named Dina Montufar-Solis, who was from Guatemala but had lived in the US for many years. She made many important contributions to the project.

Finally, my life settled down nicely. My research was moving along well, and Jeanne was wonderful. We got married in 2002, little more than a year after we started dating. We have now been married for twenty years. Many times, I think of the old saying that *The Third Time is a Charm*. Maybe it's just a quaint expression but in my case, truer words were never spoken.

I learned more about how to have a successful relationship from Jeanne than from any person in my life. In many ways she is a true Scorpio—ambitious, mysterious, and passionate. When she makes up her mind to do something, consider it done. Yet, in almost every way she is compromising and kind, practically to a fault. Even today when I ask what she wants to do, if I lay out options about something I'm considering, let's say, she usually defers to me.

Jeanne and I have traveled quite bit. Our best trips have been to Paris and to the Auvergne region in Central France, and to Italy, and Sweden, and Rio de Janeiro.

With a sense of peace in my life, I began to write again with renewed vigor. I decided to try my hand at a book of horror. While out in rural Texas one afternoon visiting Jeanne's sister, Laura, we passed an old farmhouse that was situated on a large spread of land. I also had met an old but colorful character named Charlie, who lived on the ranch next to Laura. Charlie had little education and could barely read or write. Suddenly the plot for a book emerged. It was named *The Ostermann House*; and was more closely in the genre of psychological thriller than horror. The book did well and garnered several awards, including an Eric Hoffer da Vinci Eye Award, a Killer Nashville Claymore Award Finalist Award, and was selected as Best Book of 2017 by Advice Books International.

I returned briefly to writing literary fiction with a book, *A Distant Past, An Uncertain Future*, then went back to horror again with two books. *The Visitor* is set in a small town in Minnesota. As it says on the back cover, 'You will know him by what he does, but who is he?'.

The Code takes place in the rural college town of Covington, Vermont. It deals with a group of people who are 'messing with the occult', only to find that something very dark and very dangerous has been turned loose. *The Code* won the 2022 Feathered Quill Silver Medal Award in Mystery and Suspense.

I located a literary agent to handle my books. She had quite a bit of success in the past and had good connections with New York editors, but now that she was nearing retirement, I was never quite sure how much time she was devoting to my work. More than once, I thought of the line from the Mamas and Papas song, *Creeque Alley*: "Broke busted, disgusted, agents can't be trusted." She was a sweet person, nonetheless, and I always managed to get my books published through other venues.

We adopted a cat from the animal shelter. It was listed as a survivor of cruelty. When it came to the shelter, it was riddled with fleas and malnourished. And was missing about half its teeth. The remaining teeth were loose and full of cavities. The shelter took care of the flea problem. We eventually took him to a board-certified veterinary dentist in town who suggested that the rest of his teeth be removed—they were beyond repair. It turns out that cats (and dogs) don't use their teeth much to eat except for hard food. Otherwise, they mostly just wolf down food without chewing much of it—teeth notwithstanding.

He ended up with the name Frankie after the title character Frankie Jones in one of my books. Both were survivors. He is kept as an indoor cat, but he has the run of the house. It took quite a while for him to warm up to us, but he is now comfortable in his new abode.

Jordan married Hailey, his high school sweetheart. He has a degree in geology and works for a Norwegian oil company. They have three boys and Jordan has become a first-rate chef at home. Jeanne likes to credit it to the time we all lived together when I did most of the cooking, though I am not so convinced. His father's side of the family has Louisiana Cajun roots. If you know anything about Cajuns, you know they love to eat and know how to throw a great meal together. I am sure there is a special Cajun gene for it.

Whereas my marriage to Jane in Oklahoma had been one never-ending imbroglio, my time with Jeanne has been two decades of pure delight. Most important, life is fun as hell! Yes, the third time *is* a charm—now I believe it. I am forever grateful to Dean Johnson for his matchmaking moxie. I don't know what made him think we would be a good pair, except that some people have a gift for seeing what others can't.

Jeanne is, and will always be, my soul mate.

27

Epilogue
If I Could Do It All Again

Children are into discovery. They want to figure things out for themselves. When we explain everything to them, or lead them to an answer, we short-circuit their intuitive desire for knowledge. We have given them the answer that they wanted to dig out for themselves.

It has been speculated by developmental biologists that the annoying repetitive habit of a toddler pushing a fork off a highchair is not really intended to drive parents nuts. Rather, it is a simple and astute experiment. Simply put, if a fork or spoon is knocked off the chair, will it always fall to the floor? Or sometimes, rarely but occasionally, will it just hang there in mid-air? It is a basic and fundamental experiment testing the laws of gravity in the subtle mind of a two-year-old.

Although I am no developmental biologist, I believe that children need to fail to succeed. This doesn't mean that it is better to be raised in an environment where there is no chance for success. It merely means that we often learn more from what did not go as planned than from what did.

When I was in the lab every day, I knew that most—the vast majority, in fact—of my experiments were doomed from the beginning. Basically, that's why Gerry Cole refused to pander me, and why Mike Bevan treated all of us like a bunch of stupid "twits" as he would say in his Welsh accent. Yes, we were twits. We had yet to learn how to think critically.

If someone is doing the thinking for us, a parent or a mentor, we never learn how to do it on our own. In fact, my mother was a lot like Gerry Cole and Mike Bevan because she let me learn from my failures, even if it meant being the only sheep on the stage at the Christmas pageant wearing bright red lipstick.

In fact, I have often viewed my life, the day in day out routine of it, as a great experiment. Which is not to say that life is not tedious and boring at times. It is. Like everyone, I have satisfied much of my curiosity doing very mundane things. And a few times, by pushing the limit.

If I could do it all again, would I?

Mostly.

www.ingramcontent.com/pod-product-compliance
Lightning Source LLC
Chambersburg PA
CBHW030255100526
44590CB00012B/413